4-HOUR MARATHON:
THE BULLETPROOF TRAINING GUIDE FOR BREAKING THE 4-HOUR BARRIER

THOMAS WATSON

4-HOUR MARATHON

Published internationally by Broadsea Press

4-HOUR MARATHON

Table of Contents

Preface: Who This Book Is For

First of all, thanks for purchasing the expanded and updated edition of *'4-Hour Marathon'*! The first edition has now helped thousands of runners achieve their marathon goals, which has been a great response. From conversations with readers and runners, I've taken the opportunity to revise the book's layout and spend more time focussing on the core 20-week training schedule – the objective has been to make a more concentrated and robust regime for runners to follow.

A quick note on the purpose and target audience of this book.

This book is written for anyone who is looking to run a marathon in under four hours.

If you are looking to simply run a marathon, with no specific time objective, you'll probably find some useful information inside – but you're not the target of this book.

Likewise, if you're aiming to run a three-hour marathon, I'd recommend looking elsewhere for more specific resources.

*

This book has been expressly written with a 'just under four-hour' finishing time in mind.

Why?

4-HOUR MARATHON

When I started my first marathon journey, I found the amount of information available online to be overwhelming.

For every important topic I researched in my marathon preparation (such as pace, training, longest runs, or nutrition), I'd find half-a-dozen different recommendations – often contradicting each other.

My aim with this book is to improve that signal-to-noise ratio, and map out a road-tested path to a sub-4-hr marathon. Instead of offering a generalised guide to marathons, I've targeted one specific goal – beating four hours – and worked backwards from there to create a comprehensive plan.

The training plan included in Chapter 3 gives a detailed 20-week roadmap, explaining exactly what your training regime should be every day. You are free to modify the plan to suit your own needs, of course. But the intention has been to provide something that is a focussed path to '4-hr' success, as opposed to a collection of general tips.

In the past seven years I've read practically every book worth reading on marathon running and training, and applied the knowledge within to complete dozens of marathons myself. I've since used that knowledge and expertise to develop training plans and guides through my website, which have now been downloaded and implemented by thousands of runners.

*

4-HOUR MARATHON

This book is not designed for people who have never run before.

Before commencing the training method presented in this book, you should ideally have been jogging or running for at least one year. You should be able to complete a 3 – 5 mile (5 - 8 km) run without stopping.

The principle training plan I've provided is 20 weeks long, cumulating in the marathon itself. This means that from the first week you'll be expected to run four times per week, with a seven-mile slow run at the end of the week.

If you have doubts about whether you can complete the first week, check out the complete training plan at the back of this book. Try it out – if you find it too taxing, you may wish to find a more achievable goal, and come back to the 4-hr marathon when you're ready.

Having said all of the above, there are plenty of exceptions to the rule out there. I've met loads of *outliers* – people who run their first marathon within a few months of buying a pair of running shoes. Obviously, having an athletic background helps if you're a non-runner.

So just because you haven't been pounding the pavements for years doesn't mean a four-hour marathon is out with your reach. But bear in mind, the less running experience you have, the more challenges you'll face in training and maintaining the 4-hr pace.

*

4-HOUR MARATHON

This book is for both first-time marathon runners *and* repeat offenders.

The book lays out the complete path you need to follow, from training to what gear to buy. That being said, it's unlikely that all readers will come to the table with the same amount of running experience, and that can be a problem for a comprehensive guide like this one.

For new runners, the feeling of being *overwhelmed* by so much information - and the scale of the task at hand - is quite common. For this reason, I've kept the book concise. I explain the importance and background behind the method I propose, but have tried to avoid unnecessary discussion or irrelevant information. This book is a how-to guide for success, not a *history of marathons* tome.

For the more experienced runners, I know myself that reading swathes of information you already are familiar with can feel like you're wasting your time. It doesn't matter how valid some the information is, it's easy to become impatient very quickly. I'd ask you to stick with it, or simply skip a section which is useful to beginners but which you don't need any help with (such as buying running shoes). Otherwise Chapter 3 (The Training Plan) should be followed regardless of your previous running history.

If there's anything you feel I didn't explain comprehensively enough, you'd be a total hero if you emailed me at hi@marathonhandbook.com and explained where you feel I could've done better.

Introduction

Why Four Hours?

If you took a random sample of a hundred people you know – regardless of age, fitness level, background, etc. – then the truth is that the majority of them would be capable of covering 26.2 miles on foot.

Most of them wouldn't be very fast – in fact, most of them would walk almost all the way. They'd stop for long breaks. A few of them would get injured or get too tired. Some would be physically incapable of completing the distance, but most would grumblingly manage to finish it. Most of us can walk for a long time, after all. This would just be a very long walk.

This is where marathons come in.

With marathons, the aim is to *run*.

And not just run, but run *continuously*. If you get tired, you might have to walk a little. But for most of us, the whole point of committing to a marathon is to try and run the whole thing.

But what is so significant about four hours?

It takes most well-prepared marathon runners somewhere between three and five hours to complete the course.

4-HOUR MARATHON

The average marathon finishing time is 4:21:291 (the average women's time was 4:39:09 – while it's a little slower, it is quickly catching up with the men's time).

This means that anyone breaking the four-hour benchmark is not just a marathon runner – they're a pretty good marathon runner. Over 65% of marathon runners are still on the road at the 4-hr mark. If you want to be in that top 35%, you've got train for it.

Running a marathon in under four hours means you've sustained an average pace of at least 6.55 miles per hour for 26.2 miles – it's a badge of honour that shows not just endurance, but a good level of underlying fitness and training behind it.

The four-hour benchmark has become an important line in the sand, it can be said. The difference between a 3hr 59min finishing time and 4hr 1min is a lot more than two minutes if you're a marathon runner.

I ran my first marathon in 3 hours 58mins. The first half of the marathon had been a breeze, taking me 1 hour 40 mins – I thought *"this is great, I'm going to cruise round"*.

The second half was a different story. My legs locked up, I walked for long sections and even when I ran it felt like I was running on the spot. I hit 'The Wall' (something I cover later). Every inch of my body was telling me to just stop. Somehow, I dug deep and pushed the 'over-ride' button on

---

Based on data of over 4 million finishing times. Source: https://marastats.com/marathon

what my body was telling me. Fuelled by pride and resolve, I pushed on and crossed the finish line a smidgeon under the four-hour mark.

It wasn't the most graceful marathon effort, and by the end I was running on sheer determination. I could barely get up and down the stairs in the following days, and swore I'd never do another marathon.

Needless to say, it took about a week before my enthusiasm returned and I started looking for my next marathon. My experience on my first marathon told me that I had prepared poorly, but the feeling of elation I got from finishing was addictive – I wanted to *get better* at marathons.

This started me on the path of in-depth marathon research – talking with veteran runners, trainers and physiotherapists to learn how I could improve not just my speed, but my ability to run a marathon comfortably. I adopted a more structured training approach, and have applied the lessons learned to run dozens of marathons in the years since that first attempt.

Through these experiences I've developed training plans and principles that have been downloaded thousands of times, helping many runners to achieve their goals.

The goal I have, and try to instil in others, is not just to finish a marathon in a good time, but to finish it **comfortably**. This means that at the finish line you're able to smile and enjoy the feeling of satisfaction that comes with your accomplishment.

The Importance of a Goal

Some people sign up for a marathon and immediately know what their target finish time is going to be. Many aim for under four hours.

Most of us, however, usually have a vague target, but don't want to commit to it – we tell people we'll *see how it goes*, avoiding the potential disappointment of not hitting our goals. When I am helping someone prepare for a marathon – especially first-timers – and ask them what their goals are, the answer is often an unsure 'I'll just try and finish'.

The truth is, having a specific finishing time in mind is great for your training. It gives you structure and a tangible target, something you can work around and strive towards. It snuffs out any ambiguity about what you should be focussing on, and takes any decision-making out of the equation. You devise a plan and you stick to it.

So that is how this book came about. The method presented here is specifically designed for people looking to prepare for, train and complete a marathon in under four hours. The training plan detailed here, as well as every piece of advice, has been reverse-engineered from the end-goal of a sub 4-hr time.

Many runners who aren't specific with their goals don't train smart, or don't mentally commit to their training regime. This lack of structure can lead to both too little and too much training, which ultimately will impact the likelihood of success on marathon day.

4-HOUR MARATHON

In this book, I've distilled your marathon preparation and training down to the fundamental building blocks required to run a 4-hr marathon.

There are two elements to this – building up mileage (endurance), and building up speed while running long miles (stamina).

Now you know what your target time is, we can already calculate the exact pace you will have to consistently run on the day of your marathon. Now, we can build a training plan for you that gets you up to that pace, then ensures you can comfortably maintain it for (just under) four hours come race day.

The one mandatory item you're going to need is a GPS watch, or at least a smartphone with reliable GPS, so you can accurately measure your pace in training.

A 4-hr marathon is achievable for almost anybody, but your chances of success will also depend on:

- Your level of underlying fitness,

- The amount of time you have to train,

- Being able to avoid / deal with injuries,

- Selecting a favourable marathon.

Training is not the only part of marathon preparation. You also have to check that all your gear is suitable, research your race, have race strategies for pacing, fuelling and hydrating – as well as knowing what to do if the wheels fall off (it happens to all of us at least once). To that end, I've included a lot of pre-race advice and checklists for you to follow as the big day approaches.

Chapter Summary – What's Coming Up

Here's a preview of what we're going to cover in the chapters which follow:

- **Chapter 1 – The 4-hr Method.** This chapter details the *why* of the 4-hr marathon method. You will learn why marathon pace is so important, what your 4-hr marathon pace strategy is going to be, and how to build yourself up to the required pace to begin the 4-hr marathon training method if you're not there yet.

- **Chapter 2 - Training.** Marathon training is a science, not an art – and the lessons learned from countless other runners can be de-constructed and applied to your own training. In this chapter, I describe the different types of workout which will be the building blocks of the 4-hr marathon method.

- **Chapter 3 – The 4-hr Marathon Training Plan.** In this chapter, I map out the 20-week workout regime aimed at getting you race-ready. I detail every day's activities, and discuss why 20 weeks is an appropriate length of time. I also discuss the practicalities of the training plan, and share links to download digital copies of the plan.

- **Chapter 4 - Shoes and gear.** Have the correct shoes and running gear is fundamental for success. I break down every piece of gear you need to run your marathon, and all the optional extras too. I discuss what to look for when you're buying shoes, shorts and everything else.

- **Chapter 5 – Nutrition and Hydration**. Fuel is what gets you round the race, but it comes in many different forms – and everyone's stomach is different. I discuss the various fuelling options to have before and during a race, as well as covering your fuelling strategy and how to road-test it before the race.

- **Chapter 6 - Pre-Marathon – the 4 weeks before the marathon.** In this chapter, I explain where your focus should be at various milestones – four weeks before the race, one week before the race, the night before the race and the morning of the race. We look at tapering and cross-training, diet and the mental preparation required so you get to the start-line in optimal condition.

- **Chapter 7 – During the Marathon.** The actual marathon is the culmination of all your training in one event. Here we go through what to expect on the day itself – this section contains practical advice and tips from experienced marathon runners.

- **Chapter 8 - Post-Marathon.** In this chapter, I discuss what to expect and how to minimise recovery time post-marathon – and how to retain your new level of distance running ability.

What to Expect

To close out the introduction to the book, I thought it would be appropriate to spend some time describing the task ahead of you.

The journey to the finish line of a marathon is like any great one – it's long, it requires a lot of effort and pain, there will be setbacks and failures – but there will be a transformation involved, and the reward at the end directly correlates to the amount of effort you put in.

The act of training for – and running – a marathon is a voyage of discovery, especially if it's your first.

You are pushing your body to its limits. Mentally, you will see how you react when faced with fatigue, zero motivation and continuous discomfort.

Training to run a sub 4-hr marathon requires an extra helping of discipline. You are not training your body just to finish, you are training your body to run a constant, high pace for the entirety of the 26.2 miles.

What You Should Expect in Training

Training for a marathon involves a bit of a balancing act – you have to increase your running ability over a contained period of time while avoiding over-training and injuries.

The amount of training required varies from person to person depending on their underlying fitness. Training for a marathon means going running four or five times per week. You have to get used to large parts of your schedule being committed to running. This means a few hours throughout the week, and a long run on weekends. The long runs can be especially encumbering to your personal life, as it cuts out a block of the time you'd usually have set aside for friends, family or hobbies. Bear in mind that you'll also be more tired after this run, so might not have the energy for that late-night dinner party you were invited to.

Your lifestyle will also change in order to prioritise your training. You might start to look at meals and snacks as 'fuel', and start to see TV time as 'non-running time'.

Injuries and setbacks are also so common that you should accept that they are quite likely – but rather than let them throw a spanner in your training, you should be expecting them, and have a plan in place to address them as soon as they appear.

What You Should Expect on Race Day

Your aim for the marathon should be run a constant pace throughout – I'll explain more on this point later in the book. This means that from the moment the starter pistol goes off, you are running the same speed you'll go at for the next (almost) four hours.

Given you've been tapering – that means winding down the intensity of your training – for the last few weeks, your body is going to be rested and ready to go. For at least the first few miles, you will practically float round the course. You'll find yourself buoyed by the adrenaline of the race and the atmosphere around you. You'll see a lot of runners passing you, but this is normal – remember, it's the tortoise and the hare effect. **Your competition is not other people**.

4-HOUR MARATHON

Often the hardest thing for runners in the first stages of a marathon is to *hold back*, and not let their adrenaline drive them forward. This is where you have to be disciplined enough to stick to the planned pace. *Trust me* - all that energy you hold back accumulates in your back pocket, ready to be unleashed later on.

As the race goes on you'll likely find yourself starting to feel some strain, but still be pretty comfortable. Most marathon runners tend to get the first half of the race under their belts feeling great.

It's usually somewhere after the half-way point – around the 14 to 16-mile mark - that the under-prepared and over-ambitious runners begin to flag. This might start as a slight reduction in speed, but as they go on they'll start to walk or take breaks. Around this point, if you're running a constant pace you'll find that the deluge of people passing you has stopped, and you're running alongside people, maybe passing a few.

The final six miles of the run are what really separates the prepared runners from the over-ambitious ones. This is where many runners hit **The Wall** – they've pushed themselves too far into the unknown, and now their bodies are shutting down and telling them to stop. It's a horrible sensation - one that I've experienced a couple of times and wouldn't wish on any runner. Again, if you've trained sufficiently and are running a constant pace at this point then you'll find you are passing all those people who passed you earlier. Sure, the final stages of a race get uncomfortable for everybody – the trick is to anticipate the tough times and train for them.

And it is inevitable that occasionally even the best-prepared runners have problems. You might find on the day that your legs are getting tight, or heavy, or you're feeling a new injury or blister. Again, if you can anticipate these issues then there is less chance they'll de-rail you on the day.

When it comes to the latter stages of marathons, it doesn't come down to luck. It comes down to training, preparation, strategy and discipline. That's what I hope to instil in this book – a philosophy that means when you cross the finish line, you do so with a big smile on your face - and can enjoy the after-burn effect of having completed a sub 4-hr marathon.

*

If there's anything you feel I've missed, or if you still have questions, drop me a line (hi@marathonhandbook.com) and I'll do my best to help you.

And if you've enjoyed this book, please remember to leave a review over at Amazon!

Thanks and run far,

Thomas at Marathon Handbook
hi@marathonhandbook.com

4-HOUR MARATHON

Chapter 1: The 4-hr Method

This chapter details the theory behind the 4-hr marathon method. Before getting to the method itself, I'll explain a couple of the building blocks to detail the logic.

In this chapter you'll discover:

- Why Marathon Pace Is So Important;
- The 4-Hr Marathon Target Pace;
- How to train towards the 4-hr pace;
- How conditions can affect your finishing time – and why you should pick a fast marathon.

Marathon Pace: A Primer

I would argue that your marathon pace is the most important variable within your control on the day of your marathon. It will determine whether you finish within four hours or not.

How?

When most people think about pace, they're just thinking about the actual speed they are running; 9 minutes per mile, for example.

The truth is that this isn't pace, but **instantaneous speed** – a snapshot of how fast you are running at a particular moment.

Marathon Pace is a description of the **overall speed profile** you follow **throughout** your marathon.

4-HOUR MARATHON

Most marathon runners – especially first timers – will slow down over the course of the event, particularly towards the end as fatigue kicks in.

Marathon runners track their progress using a system called '*splits*'. This is simply splitting the course into evenly-sized sections, and tracking the time to complete each 'split'. Typically, a split will be every few miles or kilometres, and many marathon events provide automatic chip-based split tracking.

Therefore, a runner's Marathon Pace can be evaluated by examining their split times.

A runner who gradually slows down throughout the race is said to have 'positive splits'.

A runner who speeds up throughout the race has 'negative splits'.

And a runner who runs a consistent pace throughout the entire marathon has '**even splits**'.

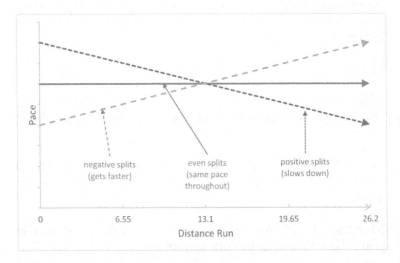

In your 4-hr marathon, your target is going to be to run 'even splits'.

In other words, **you should be aiming for a consistent pace throughout your marathon**.

Why?

Why Even Splits Is the Goal

The vast majority of marathon runners are faster in the first half than the second. In other words, they're running *positive splits* – they slow down as the race goes on.

Why is this? It's usually a combination of early-stage adrenaline, lack of pace planning, and slowing down near the end due to fatigue or injury.

These *positive splitters* often hit the wall (more on this later) and find the last few miles of their marathon particularly excruciating. They've either pushed too hard in the early stages, or haven't prepared their bodies for the 26.2 miles – or a bit of both. It happened to me on my first marathon, and in general it's the most common mistake made in marathon running.

It's very easy to do – especially when you haven't run a full marathon before, and aren't sure how to manage your pace. You're more likely to talk yourself into running faster at the start, convincing yourself you feel good and you might just be able to maintain this new speed for the full marathon.

In other words, it's a rookie mistake. And it happens all the time. At the finish line, you'll recognise the 'positive' split people – they're the ones that look completely exhausted.

The opposite of this is to run *negative splits* – this means gradually speed up throughout the race. This is the technique traditionally used by elite marathon runners. It's a conservative approach which means you are holding back for most of the race, and should ensure you have enough energy to finish strong.

The reason why negative splits aren't more popular is that most marathon runners simply are not disciplined enough to use them. Most runners prefer to 'go for broke' and see how fast they can go, as opposed to consciously holding back.

The drawback of running negative splits is that you need good knowledge of what your expected marathon performance is going to be in order to plan your pace accordingly.

And that leaves *even splits*, i.e. running a constant speed throughout the race.

This is the approach we are going to use in the 4-hr marathon method.

Why?

Even splits mean your body is running at the same pace for the entire marathon, which makes things a lot more straightforward. We can prepare your body for running at this pace in training. It will become second nature.

This means you won't be training to excessive speeds, and thus subjecting your body to unnecessary stresses which can increase the risk of injury.

I wouldn't recommend planning for negative splits if you're a marathon novice. Until your body is conditioned to run 26.2 miles consistently, it is very unlikely that you'll actually be able to maintain even splits – it's more likely that you'll begin to tail off towards the end. But as I'm about to explain, we can build a little bit of fat into the system to account for that.

The 4-Hr Marathon Target Pace

In order to get around your marathon in exactly four hours, you would need to run a 9:09min/mile pace, or 5:41min/km.

Here's the thing though – no marathon is perfect. Whether its hills, fatigue, toilet stops, crowds at the start or that old knee injury, something is likely to slow you down at some point in your run. If you're a marathon novice, it's fairly likely that you'll slow down towards the end – no matter how much you've trained to hold that consistent marathon pace.

Therefore the 4-hr marathon pace we'll be training to in Chapter 3 actually allows for 10 minutes of padding . . . thus finishing in 3hrs 50mins if all goes well.

The 4-hr Marathon Pace

The following is the speed to train to using your GPS device. Note: the below speeds give an equivalent marathon finishing time of 3hrs 50min.

8:46min/mile

5:27min/km

The above pace will be referenced throughout this book as the '4-hr Marathon Pace' (despite it being the 3hrs 50min pace).

4-HOUR MARATHON

During your marathon, it is also worth keeping the actual 4hr-marathon speeds in your mind – to make sure you don't fall below them.

It's fine to go faster than this pace, but don't go too much faster – all we want to do is finish within four hours, right? And the last thing you want to do is use up energy early on that you later really need.

For your reference, the table which follows shows marathon finishing times against the pace required to achieve it.

Target Time (hh:mm)	min / km	min / mile
06:00	08:32	13:44
05:45	08:11	13:10
05:30	07:49	12:36
05:15	07:28	12:01
05:00	07:07	11:27
04:45	06:45	10:53
04:30	06:24	10:19
04:15	06:03	9:44
04:00	05:41	9:10
03:45	05:20	8:35
03:30	04:59	8:01
03:15	04:37	7:26

How to Train Towards the 4-hr Pace

The training runs in the 20-week training method in the next chapter are designed to be done at the target marathon pace (8:46min/mile or 5:27min/km).

Therefore, we need to make sure you can complete the initial training runs at this speed. My recommendation is to check out the first week of training activities from the next chapter, and try it out.

The 20-week plan is designed to be followed once you can run 3 or 4 miles at the target pace. If you've realised that the target pace is too quick for you at the moment, in the next chapter I describe how to spend a few weeks using the Block Method to build up to the required pace.

Pick A Fast Marathon Course

The 4-hr marathon method assumes that the course conditions are going to be relatively consistent and favourable to running even splits. However, many marathons have some features – whether it's hills, wind, or crowds – that can slow you down.

The best way to mitigate against these issues is to **pick a fast marathon**.

If your goal is simply to run a sub-4hr marathon, you might as well make things as easy as possible. When it comes to running marathons, there are quite a few variables to consider that will affect your finishing time. If you haven't already decided which marathon you are going to run, try and find one with as much of the following conditions as possible:

4-HOUR MARATHON

Flat.   Gradients make your marathon training and preparation more complex.   It's not practical to maintain even splits on an undulating course.   So try and find a marathon that is as flat as possible.

Small-to-medium sized.   The huge city marathons often pack in all the non-elite runners into huge groups.   In these races, it is common for runners to spend the first 20 – 30 minutes shuffling along in the herd, before enough space is available to start to run.   There goes your 4-hr marathon attempt. Avoid this issue by choosing a small-to-medium sized marathon, or doing research on your specific race and ensuring you won't be hindered by the huge crowds. If you find yourself in a big group at the start line, don't be afraid to push to the start of your section.

Favourable, familiar climate. Hopefully your marathon is in roughly the same climate as your training conditions. You're looking for something cool, not too sticky, and windless.

Good underfoot conditions.   A marathon with softer underfoot conditions – and ones that are similar to your training – are favourable.

Accounting for Marathon Conditions

Wind, rising temperatures, hills, and other gradients all effect your comfortable running pace.   If your marathon course features any of these - a massive hill at mile 18, for example - then it has to be factored into your pacing strategy.

In the case of the 'hill at 18 miles' example, you should figure out what your comfortable pace is when running the same gradient of hill, and adjust the rest of your pace accordingly. So, if you calculate you'll lose five minutes on the hills, you should increase your pace slightly for the rest of the race in order to make up those lost five minutes.

4-HOUR MARATHON

Chapter 2: Training

In this chapter, you'll discover:

- How to assess whether you are at '4-hr marathon' training pace (and how to reach it if you're not there yet);

- The details of the different types of running and cross training you'll perform. These are the building blocks of the 20-week training plan in the next chapter.

Getting to the 4-hr Pace

The following few pages are for those runners who are not currently able to complete the first week of the 20-week training plan at the required pace.

Not sure if you're there yet?

Here's the first week of the plan:

Monday: rest
Tuesday: 3 miles @ marathon pace (8:46/mile or 5:27/km).
Wednesday: 45min speed work
Thursday: 30-60 mins of cross-training
Friday: 3 miles @ marathon pace (8:46/mile or 5:27/km).
Saturday: rest
Sunday: 7 mile Long Slow Run

Essentially, if you can run 3 miles (5) continuously at the 4-hr marathon pace, you are ready to start the 20-week plan.

For guidance on the speed work and long slow run, see later in this chapter.

If you are not at marathon pace yet, no worries – let's work on it.

What Is Your Current Physical Condition?

This is the first piece of information that needs to be established. Where are you right now, in terms of physical preparation? Wherever you are, this becomes your 'base line' to build from.

Some questions to get you thinking about your current level of readiness:

- How far can you continuously run right now at a conversational pace (holding a conversation while running)?

- When you go for a run, what is your *default* pace – the speed you naturally run at when not pushing too hard? The goal is to increase this to the 4-hr marathon pace as soon as we can.

How Long is Required to Get to 4-hr Marathon Pace?

Before you can start the 20-week programme, you have to get to marathon pace – this will take another few weeks. The length of this phase depends on your current fitness level.

What's Your Current Pace?

We've established that a 4-hr marathon should be run at a consistent speed of 8:46min/miles, or 5:27min/km. If you follow my 20-week training plan, this will also be the pace of your typical training runs.

To establish your current speed, strap on your GPS and go for a run. Try and run continuously for 30 minutes, at a sustainable pace.

Now with your current pace in mind, let's look at how to increase it to the 4-hr marathon pace.

The Block Method for Improving Speed

The following method is a form of Interval Training for improving running speed that is commonly used for novice runners. I've adapted it for the purposes of the 4-hr plan. I've called it the **Block Method**, simply because the grid we'll use looks like a bunch of building blocks.

Your goal, prior to commencing the 20-week 4-hr marathon plan, is to run for 30 minutes continuously at the 4-hr marathon pace.

Right now, you are able to run for 30 minutes, but not at the 4-hr marathon pace for the full run. In order to change this, we're going to split that 30 minutes up into 10 x 3 minute blocks:

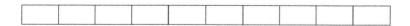

The idea is that a white block represents a 3 minute segment run at your current running pace.

A black block will represent a 3 minute interval run at 4-hr marathon pace: **8:46min/mile, or 5:27min/km.**

4-HOUR MARATHON

Therefore, the above blocks represents a 30 minute run, broken down as follows:

- 6 minutes at your current pace
- 3 minutes at 4-hr marathon pace
- 6 minutes at your current pace
- 3 minutes at 4-hr marathon pace
- 6 minutes at your current pace
- 3 minutes at 4-hr marathon pace
- 1 minute at your current pace.

The aim is that over the weeks, you increase the number of black blocks – in other words, you increase the amount of time you are running the 4-hr marathon pace, until that whole table turns black. Simple, right?

This method is effective as it's flexible for anyone to try out, regardless of their current running ability.

The speed at which you progress using the Block Method is really under your control – you should only add more black blocks when you feel ready.

Once you've got a completely black table, I'd recommend spending 2-3 weeks simply running 5kms at marathon pace to consolidate that fitness base, before embarking on the 20-week plan.

4-HOUR MARATHON

I've included an example Block Method plan as an appendix to this book.

Types of Training

Let's look at the different exercises, routines and workouts that will constitute your 'marathon training' – these will be the building blocks of your training plan.

I've split the different types of training into two categories:

- **Run Training**. Any type of training that involves putting one foot in front of the other.

- **Cross Training.** This is any kind of exercise that supports your running, without actually being running – whether it's stretching, swimming, yoga, etc.

Run Training

Simply 'going for a run' is a great way to train for a marathon. However, in order to optimise your training and make best use of your time, each run should have a purpose and form that in some way contributes to your plan. Here are the different broad categories your runs can fall into:

Training Run

For the purposes of this programme, a 'Training Run' means a run performed at the 4-hr marathon pace **(8:46min/miles, or 5:27min/km).**

These training runs are at the core of the training plan, with two per week throughout the 20-week plan.

The purpose of these training runs is to **build up your running base fitness** and add to your mileage, while also getting your body used to the 4-hr marathon pace. These runs start of at 3 miles long, and peak at 7 miles.

By running regularly at the 4-hr marathon pace for a few months, you will find it easy to fall into step with this pace at the event.

Long Runs

Long Runs are a staple of marathon training and are typically done once a week, at weekends. These long runs are your opportunity to increase your mileage as the marathon draws near, and are done at a <u>slow, comfortable pace</u>.

Run slower than marathon pace – try to always go at a speed you could comfortably hold a conversation with. The goal with long runs is to get your body used to the long hours and miles on your feet – so they are ready to tackle the 26.2 miles on race day.

If you want to measure your pace, a rough rule of thumb is to consider going at 1-2 min/mile slower than the 4-hr marathon pace. But seriously, don't get hung up on pace. The long runs are all about building up your maximum mileage and time on your feet, nothing more.

You'll notice in the 20-week training plan provided that the long run distances gradually build, but every few weeks they reduce in length.

These are 'step-back' weeks - weeks when you intentionally lower your total mileage while keeping training - the idea of these weeks is it lets you consolidate your running base fitness, before pushing to the next level.

4-HOUR MARATHON

Incorporating step-backs is a more effective (and less injury-prone) way to increase your mileage over the long-term when doing things like training for marathons.

Speed Work – Interval Training

Speed work is run training specifically designed to increase your baseline running pace. Most forms of speed work fall under the category of Interval Training, which is essentially alternating your run between fast and slow speeds.

Interval training is very common with experienced marathon runners looking to improve their finishing time. That's why we're going to use it in your 20-week plan. By including one session per week of relatively light interval training, you should gradually feel more and more comfortable maintaining the 4-hr pace as a regular baseline.

So, what should your interval training look like?

The technique we're going to use is well-proven, and are very close to 'Yasso 800s' – a classic marathon-training method for experienced runners.

The intervals will be 800m long – so you will run a fast 800m at the pace specified (or as near to it as you can get), then cover 800m very slowly – just a slow jog or even a walk to recover. Repeat this fast/slow process as many times as the training plan specifies (week 1 starts with 3 repeats, and the max is 10 repeats)

The pace specified for the 'fast' intervals is around 1 min / mile faster than the '4-hr marathon pace. In other words, it should be uncomfortable but hopefully not unbearable.

Therefore, interval training for the 20-week plan should look like this (note: a GPS device is essential):

1.   Warm up slow run for 2-5 minutes

2.   Run 800m at 7:42min/mile / 4:47min/km

3.   Run or walk 800m

4.   Repeat steps 2 and 3 as per training plan.

Races

A common question is 'should I do other races in preparation for my marathon?' Although you don't want to over-do it or interrupt your training schedule too much with other running commitments.

However, if there happens to be races in your area which roughly map on to the distances you had planned on your training programme, then go for it! Of particular use can be a half-marathon, 4-8 weeks before your marathon, to help gauge your pace, get you used to racing and compliment your training.

Cross Training

Cross training is any kind of non-running workout that compliments your marathon training.

Unfortunately, cross training can be the first item to be dismissed from your training plan when real life gets in the way and you realise you don't have all the time in the world to prepare for your race – and you want to spend all your available time out running.

The truth is that cross training is not mandatory – many successful marathon runners do well with absolutely zero cross training. The benefits of cross training, however – injury prevention, retaining flexibility, giving your body recovery time – are positive enough that it comes highly recommended if you can find the time.

While preparing for your marathon, you don't want to do any sports or activities that could cause injury or negatively affect your performance – so contact sports should be out. Running also pulls your body in a different direction from many physical sports – running can limit your flexibility, and the amount of cardio you do in your training will invariably lead to weight loss.

Likewise, it's probably not wise to introduce totally new forms of exercise to your body just in the name of cross-training. If you've never lifted a dumb-bell in your life, the weeks prior to your first marathon are probably not the optimal time to start.

Even if you choose not to incorporate any cross-training into your training plan, you may wish to schedule a few sessions as your marathon approaches and you are winding down your run training – this'll help to keep your body agile and ready for race day.

Here are some popular forms of cross training, and how they can complement your marathon training:

4-HOUR MARATHON

Swimming

Swimming is a great minimal-impact cardio activity that you can do as cross-training, or even sneak in a few easy laps on your rest days. The gentle pressure of the water gives your muscles a mini-massage, and being in the pool lets you fully stretch out in ways you otherwise can't. It's a great way to 'reset' a fatigued body, while giving a cardio workout at the same time. Depending on your ability, I'd recommend 30-60 minutes of pool time once a week as cross training.

Gym / Bodyweight exercises

A seasoned runner can turn themselves into an injury-proof, all-round athletic machine by dedicating a few work-outs per week to the gym. Most running injuries occur due to weaknesses, misalignments and imbalances – the easiest way to mitigate against these is strength training.

Spending just one hour per week on a 'leg day', focussing on glutes and hamstrings will do your lower body the world of good. You can even do your 'leg day' at home with free-standing squats and lunges.

The problem is factoring a 'leg day' into your marathon training plan – leg days leave your legs stiff, tired and in need of some recovery time. So, while you're deep into your marathon training, keep the weights low and the reps at a comfortable number – this will let your leg muscles get a workout to help condition them without pushing them to fatigue.

And why stop at legs once you're in the gym? The core, back, chest, shoulders, arms – all of these are used when running, so why not strengthen them up too? The upper body strength improves your overall form and technique, making it easier to keep running those last few miles on those long days.

Even a simple body-weight circuit of press-up variations, pull-ups, free standing squats and dips can give your upper body a comprehensive work-out.

Rest Days

Giving your body the time to recuperate is super important – it wards of any potential injuries, allows your muscles to relax and for you to mentally take a day off from your training too. The 20-week training plan allows for two rest days per week.

The amount of rest days you need depends on your underlying fitness level – if you're already doing some form of exercise seven days a week, then you probably just need one day to recuperate after working your legs so hard.

If, however, like most of us, your marathon training plan represents a big step-up in the amount of physical activity you usually do, then your body needs time to adjust. In this case, taking two rest days per week is totally acceptable.

Taking more than two rest days per week is fine if you're feeling really tired, but you are beginning to eat into your marathon preparation – so I recommend not taking more than two unless you feel you need it. If your legs are too tired or sore to train one day, then perhaps look at doing cross-training such as swimming or gym work rather than just skipping your workout entirely.

4-HOUR MARATHON

Keeping yourself disciplined is key to marathon success, and if you start to deviate from your training plan then it can be a slippery slope that leads to you being unfit to complete your marathon comfortably.

The Art of Tapering

First off, why taper?

U.S. mountain-running champion Nicole Hunt sums it up as follows:

Tapering helps *"bolster muscle power, increase muscle glycogen, muscle repair, freshen the mind, fine-tune the neural network so that it's working the most efficiently, and most importantly, eliminate the risk of overtraining where it could slow the athlete down the most . . .studies have indicated that a taper can help runners improve by 6 to 20%"*

The length of your taper depends on your underlying athletic ability, and the amount of training you typically do. If you have been running half-marathons every weekend for years, then there's little need to taper for more than a few days prior to the race.

If, however, this is your first marathon and you've really stretched the limits of your body during tapering, 3-4 weeks is recommended to get your body into peak race-day condition.

4-HOUR MARATHON

Tapering Checklist:

- Mileage. Each week of your taper you should decrease your weekly mileage by 20-35%.

- Pace. Your runs should be a gradually decreasing intensity.

- Long Runs. These should decrease in length significantly…by 30-40% each week.

- Speed workouts. In these final few weeks, your race day potential is already locked in – anything you do now to try and increase your athletic abilities will likely work against you on marathon day. For this reason, there is no speed work in the last two weeks of the 20-week plan.

- Conditions. Avoid steep hills, rough terrain or anything unnecessarily challenging that could lead to injury.

- For more details on physical, mental and logistical preparation four weeks before your race, check out Chapter 6: Before the Marathon.

Chapter 3: The 4-hr Marathon

Training Plan

This chapter is dedicated to presenting the complete 4-hr marathon training plan, broken down week-by-week.

If you're not already at the 4-hr marathon pace in your training runs, refer to the previous chapter for how to improve your running speed before embarking on the 20-week plan.

Training Plan Download

The complete plan is available on a single page in the appendix of this book, and online at www.marathonhandbook.com/4hrs .

Using the above link, you can download both PDF and Excel versions of the plan. I've shared the Excel version so you may customise the training plan to suit your needs – such as moving around rest days, or adding in your personal commitments.

A note on units: I have used miles predominantly throughout this book and the training plan which follows. However, I've also included the same training plan converted to kilometres both in the appendix of this book and on my website, at the link above!

Why 20 Weeks?

The 4-hr Marathon Training Method is presented as a 20-week plan.

Twenty weeks should be sufficient time to build up the required endurance and stamina levels. It allows time to build up your base of distance and speed, then to peak a few weeks before the marathon and enter into the 'taper' period. Anything much longer than this increases the amount of time your body is put under increased stress, and exponentially increases the risk of injury and / or burnout.

Some Practical Notes on The Training Plan

Before we begin, let me discuss a few practical points on the training plan provided.

The days of the week of the training plan are flexible, but the order of the exercises is not. In other words, if you plan to do your cross-training at your regular spin class on Monday, don't keep your Long Runs on Sundays. Move them accordingly.

The plan is structured strategically to take maximum advantage of rest days between activities.

In the plan, Long Runs have been scheduled for Sundays. This is simply because in my experience, runners find Sunday mornings to be the easiest and most practical time to go for a long training run. They have free time, and the rest of the day to recover.

Since Long Runs are on Sundays, Mondays are automatically rest days to allow the body to recover.

Then come Tuesday, your body will be ready to get going again with a Training Run – followed by Speed Work on Wednesday.

Thursday allows an opportunity for a mid-week cross training session to switch things up, before another Training Run on Friday.

After four days of activity, Saturday is a good day for a rest day – and many runners find it a good day to catch up on personal commitments too.

This routine is designed to push your body's comfortable endurance and stamina limits every week, with enough rest days to allow you to recharge your batteries.

Of course, you are free to adapt the plan as much as you please (download an Excel version at www.marathonhandbook.com/4hrs), but bear in mind the logic I've followed above.

The 20-Week Training Plan

Week 1

	Exercise	Details
Monday	Rest Day	
Tuesday	Training Run	3 miles / 5km 8:46min/mile / 5:27min/km
Wednesday	Speed Work	3 x 800m intervals 7:42min/mile / 4:47min/km
Thursday	Cross Training	30 – 60 mins
Friday	Training Run	3 miles / 5km 8:46min/mile / 5:27min/km
Saturday	Rest Day	
Sunday	Long Run	7 miles / 11km Slow, conversational pace
	Mileage:	16 miles / 26 km

This week is all about setting off on the right foot, adopting the training plan and getting started.

Download and print off the training plan from the link noted earlier and stick it somewhere visible – on your wall, on the fridge – somewhere you'll see it and track it every day.

Your first run on Tuesday should be focussed on running at the 4-hr marathon pace and getting used to maintaining that speed using your GPS.

4-HOUR MARATHON

Week 2

	Exercise	Details
Monday	Rest Day	
Tuesday	Training Run	3 miles / 5km 8:46min/mile / 5:27min/km
Wednesday	Speed Work	3 x 800m intervals 7:42min/mile / 4:47min/km
Thursday	Cross Training	30 – 60 mins
Friday	Training Run	3 miles / 5km 8:46min/mile / 5:27min/km
Saturday	Rest Day	
Sunday	Long Run	8 miles / 13km Slow, conversational pace
	Mileage:	17 miles / 28 km

For many runners, the thing they struggle with most in the 20-week plan is the Long Run. It is farther than they've covered by foot in the past.

A reminder: the objective of the long run is simply to cover that mileage on foot. The pace is pretty irrelevant. If you have loads of energy, then run it at 60-90 seconds per mile slower than the 4-hr marathon pace. But likewise, if you're struggling, stop and walk. That's ok!

On Sundays, it's all about building miles on your feet, not speed.

4-HOUR MARATHON

Week 3

	Exercise	Details
Monday	Rest Day	
Tuesday	Training Run	3 miles / 5km 8:46min/mile / 5:27min/km
Wednesday	Speed Work	4 x 800m intervals 7:42min/mile / 4:47min/km
Thursday	Cross Training	30 – 60 mins
Friday	Training Run	3 miles / 5km 8:46min/mile / 5:27min/km
Saturday	Rest Day	
Sunday	Long Run	9miles / 14.5km Slow, conversational pace
	Mileage:	19 miles / 30.5 km

If you haven't already, this week is a good time to identify the pair of shoes you'll run the marathon with.

If, after a couple of weeks of training, you're having doubts about your running shoes, get to a shoe store and find a better pair – the longer you leave it, the worse it'll get. See Chapter 4 for my guide to finding the right pair of marathon shoes.

4-HOUR MARATHON

Week 4

	Exercise	Details
Monday	Rest Day	
Tuesday	Training Run	4 miles / 6.5 km 8:46min/mile / 5:27min/km
Wednesday	Speed Work	4 x 800m intervals 7:42min/mile / 4:47min/km
Thursday	Cross Training	30 – 60 mins
Friday	Training Run	4 miles / 6.5 km 8:46min/mile / 5:27min/km
Saturday	Rest Day	
Sunday	Long Run	6 miles / 9.5km Slow, conversational pace
	Mileage:	18 miles / 28.5 km

This week is the first 'step-back' week, which is where your Long Run is a little shorter than previous weeks. This occasional 'step-back' is designed to give your body a pause from the relentless increase of mileage, and consolidate the improvements in stamina and endurance which you've made over the previous weeks.

4-HOUR MARATHON

Week 5

	Exercise	Details
Monday	Rest Day	
Tuesday	Training Run	4 miles / 6.5 km 8:46min/mile / 5:27min/km
Wednesday	Speed Work	5 x 800m intervals 7:42min/mile / 4:47min/km
Thursday	Cross Training	30 – 60 mins
Friday	Training Run	4 miles / 6.5 km 8:46min/mile / 5:27min/km
Saturday	Rest Day	
Sunday	Long Run	11 miles / 17.5 km Slow, conversational pace
	Mileage:	24 miles / 37 km

If you haven't already, now is a good time to start experimenting with different forms of sports nutrition. Come marathon day, you'll have to keep your body driving forward for (almost) four hours without stopping. To do this, you need fuel.

Gels are the most common source of energy for marathon runners - I talk about them more in Chapter 5. They're not for everyone, and everyone has different dietary preferences, so it's never too early to start planning out what you're going to bring with you, and what your fuelling strategy is going to be.

4-HOUR MARATHON

Week 6

	Exercise	Details
Monday	Rest Day	
Tuesday	Training Run	4 miles / 6.5 km 8:46min/mile / 5:27min/km
Wednesday	Speed Work	5 x 800m intervals 7:42min/mile / 4:47min/km
Thursday	Cross Training	30 – 60 mins
Friday	Training Run	4 miles / 6.5 km 8:46min/mile / 5:27min/km
Saturday	Rest Day	
Sunday	Long Run	12 miles / 19 km Slow, conversational pace
	Mileage:	25 miles / 40 km

Week 6 is the same workload as last week, with a slightly longer Long Run.

As your training intensifies, it's worth remembering that the body needs time to recover. This means allowing more time for sleeping and resting up!

It's a common mistake to increase your training dramatically and try and continue with the rest of your life as normal. This is a dangerous path, as not enough rest can lead to fatigue, burnout, injury and illness . . .just what you want to avoid when training for a marathon.

4-HOUR MARATHON

Week 7

	Exercise	Details
Monday	Rest Day	
Tuesday	Training Run	5miles / 8 km 8:46min/mile / 5:27min/km
Wednesday	Speed Work	6 x 800m intervals 7:42min/mile / 4:47min/km
Thursday	Cross Training	30 – 60 mins
Friday	Training Run	5 miles / 8 km 8:46min/mile / 5:27min/km
Saturday	Rest Day	
Sunday	Long Run	9 miles / 14.5 km Slow, conversational pace
	Mileage:	25 miles / 40.5 km

This week is another 'step-back' week – the long run is 3 miles (or 5km) shorter than last week, so enjoy the easier Sunday!

At the same time, your Training Runs and Speed work have increased slightly, so the overall weekly mileage doesn't change.

4-HOUR MARATHON

Week 8

	Exercise	Details
Monday	Rest Day	
Tuesday	Training Run	5miles / 8 km 8:46min/mile / 5:27min/km
Wednesday	Speed Work	6 x 800m intervals 7:42min/mile / 4:47min/km
Thursday	Cross Training	30 – 60 mins
Friday	Training Run	5 miles / 8 km 8:46min/mile / 5:27min/km
Saturday	Rest Day	
Sunday	Long Run	15 miles / 24 km Slow, conversational pace
	Mileage:	31 miles / 50 km

A jump in mileage this week . . . on your Long Run, you'll cross the half-marathon distance for the first time – great work!

Another first is that your weekly mileage is now more than the length of a complete marathon.

4-HOUR MARATHON

Week 9

	Exercise	Details
Monday	Rest Day	
Tuesday	Training Run	5 miles / 8 km 8:46min/mile / 5:27min/km
Wednesday	Speed Work	7 x 800m intervals 7:42min/mile / 4:47min/km
Thursday	Cross Training	30 – 60 mins
Friday	Training Run	5 miles / 8 km 8:46min/mile / 5:27min/km
Saturday	Rest Day	
Sunday	Long Run	16 miles / 26 km Slow, conversational pace
	Mileage:	33 miles / 53 km

Long Runs can be a source of meditation-like zen for some runners, boredom for others. During a marathon training programme, I typically run with audiobooks or podcasts during my Long Runs.

I also try and pick new and exciting routes to get the miles in – even if it means driving some distance from home.

Long Runs can be a hassle, or an opportunity.

4-HOUR MARATHON

Week 10

	Exercise	Details
Monday	Rest Day	
Tuesday	Training Run	6 miles / 9.5 km 8:46min/mile / 5:27min/km
Wednesday	Speed Work	7 x 800m intervals 7:42min/mile / 4:47min/km
Thursday	Cross Training	30 – 60 mins
Friday	Training Run	6 miles / 9.5 km 8:46min/mile / 5:27min/km
Saturday	Rest Day	
Sunday	Half Marathon	13.1 miles / 21.1km Slow, conversational pace
	Mileage:	32 miles / 51 km

Another step-back week – this week, your Long Run is a half marathon, done at the usual slow pace.

If you can find an actual half marathon event in your area this weekend, it's a great opportunity to get used to the race environment and test out your gear. Just don't get carried away with your pace – remember, you're simply looking to complete the mileage.

4-HOUR MARATHON

Week 11

	Exercise	Details
Monday	Rest Day	
Tuesday	Training Run	6 miles / 9.5 km 8:46min/mile / 5:27min/km
Wednesday	Speed Work	8 x 800m intervals 7:42min/mile / 4:47min/km
Thursday	Cross Training	30 – 60 mins
Friday	Training Run	6 miles / 9.5 km 8:46min/mile / 5:27min/km
Saturday	Rest Day	
Sunday	Long Run	17 miles / 27 km Slow, conversational pace
	Mileage:	37 miles / 59 km

Congratulations – you've made it past the half-way point of this training plan!

This week sees another increase in overall mileage, so as always remember to take it slow on the long run, and don't be afraid to pull a rest day if your body is telling you it's time to cut back.

The speed work this week is up to eight intervals, which gets tough – but really helps build that endurance that will help drive you for four hours on your marathon day.

4-HOUR MARATHON

Week 12

	Exercise	Details
Monday	Rest Day	
Tuesday	Training Run	6 miles / 9.5 km 8:46min/mile / 5:27min/km
Wednesday	Speed Work	8 x 800m intervals 7:42min/mile / 4:47min/km
Thursday	Cross Training	30 – 60 mins
Friday	Training Run	6 miles / 9.5 km 8:46min/mile / 5:27min/km
Saturday	Rest Day	
Sunday	Long Run	18 miles / 29 km Slow, conversational pace
	Mileage:	38 miles / 61 km

Recovery is key to a well-executed training plan. And as you increase the mileage, you have to be smart at recovering quickly enough.

Some of my tips are as follows:

Eat something soon after your longer runs to help fuel your recovery. A protein-rich meal is perfect.

Elevate your legs. Your marathon training plan is the perfect excuse for you to sit around with your legs up every evening. It helps you recover, and you've earned it.

Massages (self-administered or otherwise) really help. I use a foam roller and trigger point ball.

Finally, if you have access to some kind of cold-water plunge pool or ice-bath, I've found these extremely beneficial in aiding my recovery times.

4-HOUR MARATHON

Week 13

	Exercise	Details
Monday	Rest Day	
Tuesday	Training Run	6 miles / 9.5 km 8:46min/mile / 5:27min/km
Wednesday	Speed Work	9 x 800m intervals 7:42min/mile / 4:47min/km
Thursday	Cross Training	30 – 60 mins
Friday	Training Run	6 miles / 9.5 km 8:46min/mile / 5:27min/km
Saturday	Rest Day	
Sunday	Long Run	14 miles / 22.5 km Slow, conversational pace
	Mileage:	35 miles / 60 km

Another step-back week, which I'm sure you'll welcome!

Remember that step-back weeks are an important part of the overall training plan, so if you're feeling strong don't be tempted to push it too hard or increase the pace of your Long Run . . . stick to the plan and your body will thank you!

4-HOUR MARATHON

Week 14

	Exercise	Details
Monday	Rest Day	
Tuesday	Training Run	6 miles / 9.5 km 8:46min/mile / 5:27min/km
Wednesday	Speed Work	9 x 800m intervals 7:42min/mile / 4:47min/km
Thursday	Cross Training	30 – 60 mins
Friday	Training Run	6 miles / 9.5 km 8:46min/mile / 5:27min/km
Saturday	Rest Day	
Sunday	Long Run	20 miles / 32 km Slow, conversational pace
	Mileage:	41 miles / 65.5 km

The miles are building up this week, and the Long Run hits 20 miles. This will be your second-longest run before the marathon (the longest one is in two weeks).

There's always a debate about the appropriate distance of the longest training run before a marathon. For the average runner, marathon training means a huge ramp up in their mileage – this runs the risk of injury and overtraining. So, there's a balance between planning a sufficient number and distance of long runs, and not over-doing it.

This week you'll run a 20-mile long run, and in two weeks a 21 miler. These will get your body into that groove of running for 3+ hrs continuously, without (hopefully) pushing it too far. We can save that possibility for marathon day, when you're going to give it your all!

4-HOUR MARATHON

Week 15

	Exercise	Details
Monday	Rest Day	
Tuesday	Training Run	7 miles / 11 km 8:46min/mile / 5:27min/km
Wednesday	Speed Work	10 x 800m intervals 7:42min/mile / 4:47min/km
Thursday	Cross Training	30 – 60 mins
Friday	Training Run	7 miles / 11 km 8:46min/mile / 5:27min/km
Saturday	Rest Day	
Sunday	Sub 2hr Half Marathon	13.1 miles / 21.1 km 8:46min/mile / 5:27min/km
	Mileage:	37 miles / 59 km

This week is pretty intense.

The speed work is now up to 10 interval repeats, which is both a lot of work and time consuming.

Then your goal for the long run on Sunday is to run a half marathon at the 4-hr marathon pace. If you've followed the training plan this far, you'll probably be surprised how well you do in the half marathon.

The half marathon is included here to get you running a long distance at the 4-hr marathon pace. Remember, your goal here is simply to maintain that pace – so you should finish the half-marathon in under two hours. You can run a real half marathon, if you can find one in your area.

This is also a good opportunity to do your 'dress rehearsal' (see Chapter 6) – this is a long run done in the exact same gear and conditions that you'll experience on marathon day.

4-HOUR MARATHON

Week 16

	Exercise	Details
Monday	Rest Day	
Tuesday	Training Run	7 miles / 11 km 8:46min/mile / 5:27min/km
Wednesday	Speed Work	10 x 800m intervals 7:42min/mile / 4:47min/km
Thursday	Cross Training	30 – 60 mins
Friday	Training Run	7 miles / 11 km 8:46min/mile / 5:27min/km
Saturday	Rest Day	
Sunday	Long Run	21 miles / 34 km Slow, conversational pace
	Mileage:	45 miles / 72 km

This week is your highest mileage week of the entire training plan – after this, you will begin to taper and can take the foot off the pedal a bit.

Keep this in mind throughout this week, because motivation and fatigue may be setting in.

Remember that taking rest is sometimes the most important part of a training regime, so if you need to skip cross training or Friday's run, allow yourself to do so.

And the long run on Sunday is your longest training run. Remember – as always, the goal is to complete the miles, not to run at a good speed.

4-HOUR MARATHON

Week 17

	Exercise	Details
Monday	Rest Day	
Tuesday	Training Run	5 miles / 8 km 8:46min/mile / 5:27min/km
Wednesday	Speed Work	8 x 800m intervals 7:42min/mile / 4:47min/km
Thursday	Cross Training	30 – 60 mins
Friday	Training Run	5 miles / 8 km 8:46min/mile / 5:27min/km
Saturday	Rest Day	
Sunday	Long Run	15 miles / 24 km Slow, conversational pace
	Mileage:	33 miles / 53 km

Congratulations – you've made it to the taper!

The taper is all about conserving the endurance and stamina you've built up over the last few months.   In the last few weeks before the marathon, there's little you can do to actually improve your running fitness – the time for that is past.   Now it's all about preservation, to get you to the start line in the best possible condition.

The taper gradually reduces your running load, so this week is a good deal less intense that previous weeks.

Enjoy it, remember to rest if you're feeling burnt out after last week's high mileage, and remind yourself you're in the home straight!

4-HOUR MARATHON

Week 18

	Exercise	Details
Monday	Rest Day	
Tuesday	Training Run	4 miles / 6.5 km 8:46min/mile / 5:27min/km
Wednesday	Speed Work	4 x 800m intervals 7:42min/mile / 4:47min/km
Thursday	Cross Training	30 – 60 mins
Friday	Training Run	4miles / 6.5 km 8:46min/mile / 5:27min/km
Saturday	Rest Day	
Sunday	Long Run	12 miles / 19 km Slow, conversational pace
	Mileage:	24 miles / 38 km

The taper continues this week, as every run gets a little less intense.

You may find that your pace in the Long Runs has started to creep up. This is mainly down to your training, but also often a bit of a mental game – once you have more confidence in your ability to run a certain distance, you tend to run a bit faster.

Enjoy the taper!

4-HOUR MARATHON

Week 19

	Exercise	Details
Monday	Rest Day	
Tuesday	Training Run	3 miles / 5 km 8:46min/mile / 5:27min/km
Wednesday	Rest Day	
Thursday	Cross Training	30 – 60 mins
Friday	Training Run	3 miles / 5 km 8:46min/mile / 5:27min/km
Saturday	Rest Day	
Sunday	Long Run	8 miles / 13 km Slow, conversational pace
	Mileage:	14 miles / 23 km

Another taper week, as we continue to slow things down.

Remember that during your taper, you're not actually improving your running ability at all – you're simply preserving it. With that in mind, there's no more speed work for you – Wednesday of this week is an additional rest day.

Use this week to review and finalise all your marathon plans – hotels, transport, packing, and so on – if you haven't already.

4-HOUR MARATHON

Week 20

	Exercise	Details
Monday	Rest Day	
Tuesday	Training Run	3 miles / 5km 8:46min/mile / 5:27min/km
Wednesday	Rest Day	
Thursday	Short Run	3 miles / 5km Slow, conversational pace
Friday	Rest Day	
Saturday	Short Run	2 miles / 3.5km Slow, conversational pace
Sunday	The 4-hr Marathon!	26.2 miles / 42.2 km 8:46min/mile / 5:27min/km
	Mileage:	34.2 miles / 55.7 km

The big week is finally here!

The focus for this week is simply to go for short, simple runs to keep your legs mobile without pushing it.

On Thursday and Saturday, the idea is just to go for some short, 10-15 min runs.

Remember to carb load this week (more on that later in the book) and ensure you get a great sleep on **Friday night**, not just Saturday night.

Avoid any sources of potential illness like the plague – you have a start line to get to!

Chapter 4: Shoes & Gear

Choosing Running Shoes

Running shoes are your most important piece of race gear.

Finding a good pair of running shoes can be a minefield of questionable advice, science, marketing and hype. Here I cut through the noise and tell you how to find the shoes for you.

In this section, we'll look at:

- How to establish your criteria for your running shoes;
- What you need from a running store and its staff;
- What to look for when you try on the shoe;
- What the experts, shop workers and experienced runners look for;
- Running shoe advice specifically for beginners;
- Different shoe trends.

For those who like things summarized, here's the main findings from the next few pages:

- Be clear in what you are going to use the shoe for before you hit the stores;
- Finding a good shoe store and knowledgeable, helpful staff is paramount;
- **Comfort trumps every other variable**. Regardless of gait, pronation, foot shape, etc., how comfortable you find the shoe is a strong correlator to the chances of

avoiding injury and having a shoe you are happy with for many miles;

- Try on the shoes, spend time in them and beware of sales and marketing. Specifics of what to look for when trying shoes is detailed below;

- Gait analysis and other tools are useful – BUT they are only of value if the store person knows how to interpret them. **Gait analysis / foot type alone isn't enough to recommend a running shoe**. These are tools that can help guide you to the most appropriate shoe;

- If you're a beginner, stick to the most common and popular shoes. The average beginner runner shouldn't go for anything too extreme or exotic (barefoot, maximalist) – stick to the popular, tried and tested brands.

The short answer to 'which shoes should I buy?' is **whatever shoes you feel comfortable running in**. However, finding that pair of shoes might not be that straight-forward. Let's dive in:

Buying Running Shoes Is Not an Exact Science

This is the most important point. There's no 'perfect' shoe out there that fits everybody's feet and suits everyone's running style. There's no exact formula to follow that will lead you to your ideal shoe. It's trial and error, and as your body and running gait develop, your shoe requirements will change.

Your goal is to find a pair of shoes amongst the many that helps you achieve your running goals, keeping you happy for many miles while not getting you injured.

(Remember to look at changing your running shoes after around 500 miles.)

How Will You Use Your Running Shoes?

The first thing you want to be clear on is what your running shoe requirements are. It might sound obvious at first, but taking the time to think about your needs will make it easier to choose the right pair of shoes.

This will be important in selecting the type and various features of the shoe, and will be useful to tell the assistant at the running store when you go and start your search.

Things to consider:

- You're about to run a marathon in a few months. Make this clear to the store assistant – you're looking for a shoe that will take you through your training and the marathon.
- What's your running shoe experience and history, if you have any? Did that pair of New Balance you had fit you perfectly? Great! You can start to explore similar models. Did those cushioned shoes leave you with shin splints? OK good, we know what to avoid.

Choose a Good Running Store

A good running store with interested, knowledgeable staff is worth its weight in gold. Discount sports stores will give you just that – a discounted experience. Brand stores will have the latest shoes, but won't have the range of brands, or quite likely the knowledgeable staff to help you.

So, unless you already know exactly the type of shoes you need, head to a running store that sells several brands of shoes. You can probably find one in your area simply by Googling it.

Once inside, the staff will be able to guide you in choosing running shoes. A good running store assistant will want to know a host of information before looking at a good shoe for you – your running experience, your current mileage, injury history (what it is, where it is, what aggravates it) and shoe history.

Trying on Running Shoes

The one way to truly know that a shoe works for you is to try it out.

Before you visit the store:

- Take your running socks with you. If you don't have a pair, look to buy socks in the store – then use these when trying on running shoes. Some running stores provide socks for trying the shoes, but you should be using the socks you plan to run with.
- If you use orthotics, insoles, or thick socks with your shoes normally, bring them with you when testing shoes.
- Ladies, don't forget a sports bra as the gait analysis will have a bit of running.

Some tips for trying and buying running shoes in a shop:

- **Comfort is king**. More than any other possible factor, a shoe that feels right is the one for you. If a shoe rubs or irritates you in the store, that will only get exponentially worse when you go out for a run with them.

- Don't assume you know your size. Every brand varies slightly. You want a thumb-space between the longest toe and the shoe box. This avoids the repetitive motion of the toe hitting the toebox, which leads to sore toes / lost toenails. At the same time, if the shoe is too big your foot will move inside it and your toes will strike the toebox anyway – so it's important to find the correct size in the middle of these two situations.

- The shoes should not give friction, pain, discomfort or feel too solid / hard. If you experience any of these, this isn't the shoe for you.

- Overall feel. Get up and walk around, if the shop has some little ramps go and see how the feet move inside the shoes when going up and down hills.

- Trial them. You should always try running with the shoes on, preferably not on the treadmill – but occasionally this in unavoidable.

- In the end, listen to your gut – don't buy a shoe you don't feel 100% comfortable in. If the staff aren't listening to your needs, you can find another store.

There is a myriad of different foot shapes – narrow feet, flat feet, narrow ankles, major pronation, etc. that would be too extensive to cover here. A good store assistant will take these into account and be able to steer you towards suitable options.

A note on in-store running analysis. Many running stores use tools to analyse your foot shape and running style, before recommending a shoe. These tools can be helpful in guiding you towards the best shoe, but like any tool, it's only as good as the person using it. "A fool with a tool is still a fool".

The trick is to find a good running store with an experienced assistant to help you. Poorer running store staff simply sort everyone into one of three categories – under-pronators, over-pronators, and neutral – and recommend shoes based on this one variable. The truth is that your pronation is an important part of your foot dynamics, but doesn't tell the full story. My approach for weeding out the good from the bad is just to ask questions about pronation and how they use it to arrive at a decision– if the shop assistant gives a throwaway answer, or starts to fall apart, you know to look elsewhere.

How Many Pairs of Shoes?

Once you've found a pair of shoes that suits you, buy at least one more pair. Running shoes gradually lose their support and springiness with use, so it's worthwhile to have one relatively new pair ready to go on marathon day.

If you're simply following the 20-week plan, two pairs of shoes are sufficient. Simply train for the first 16 weeks with the first pair, and then in the final four weeks start rotating between the two pairs. This will break in the second pair (the pair you'll wear during the marathon) without wearing them out.

If you already have a pair of running shoes, or your training is going to last more than 20 weeks, consider buying three pairs – rotate the first two pairs throughout training, and in the final month include the third pair (the 'marathon shoes') in the rota.

Going Minimalist

Minimalist shoes are shoes with very little cushioning (such as Vibram Five-Fingers, Nike Frees) intended to mimic the act of running barefoot.

Minimal-style running is, in theory, better for your feet – they can develop more strength and agility, and in turn help you develop a better running gait.

However, for the vast majority of us, our bodies are just not used to the kind of movement and stresses that minimal running subjects us to. We're used to walking around in comfortable shoes and have probably learned to run in cushioned trainers – so to suddenly shed all that cushioning and support can be inviting trouble.

The key to running in minimalist shoes is a slow transition period and a very gradual increase in mileage – the lack of cushioning really does make things a lot harder when you're starting to run on empty. If you are just starting out and want to try barefoot running, I'd recommend you get into it gradually, and consider alternating between a minimal shoe with a more traditional running shoe. If you are running a marathon in a few months, you probably don't have the time to transition successfully to minimalist footwear.

Which Shoe Brands to Consider?

There's such a wide variety of running shoes available, and with new releases all the time, please visit the 'Resources' section of MarathonHandbook.com for my latest marathon shoe recommendations.

Running Socks

Socks are easily overlooked, but they are the second most important piece of kit to get right after your shoes. Poor sock choice can lead to all kinds of foot issues. Here's what to consider when choosing socks:

Avoiding Blisters

Blisters need three things to propagate – heat, friction and moisture. You can minimise moisture by **using socks designed to 'wick' away sweat**, and you can avoid friction by buying **socks that fit your feet well**, so they don't fold or clump up and lead to rubbing.

Another tip for avoiding friction is to coat the blister-prone part of your feet with a **lubricant** like Bodyglide. Vaseline works well too, but make sure to use it sparsely – it can otherwise create a little ball of all the debris in your shoe.

Toe Socks

Toe socks (such as *Injinji's*) have become increasingly popular in distance-running circles – they're the socks that are like gloves, with a separate little section for each of your toes. By isolating each individual toe, they eliminate the risk of toes rubbing together and creating blisters in that region.

Double Layers

Double-layered socks can reduce friction, thereby reducing the chances of blisters – but properly prepared feet should do this anyway. Double layered socks are obviously thicker than regular socks, which some people dislike.

Sock Height

Ankle socks are the best style for distance running, and most running socks will be roughly ankle-length. Shorter socks can bunch up under the foot, and long socks can absorb sweat and water, and sag around the ankles – becoming less comfortable as the race goes on.

Compression

Socks with **compression** sections built in are also becoming popular. These snug sections can help reduce discomfort and swelling. A lot of people prefer the feel of compression socks, so it is something to consider.

Dress Rehearsal

Don't take new, un-tested socks to a race. Always try them out somewhere first. You never know when a differently-placed seam will start to irritate your skin after a few kilometres.

Running Shirts

By-and-large you shouldn't have to over-analyse your running shirt choice - but as always, I like to look at all the factors that can play a part in selecting gear. Here are our key points when selecting a shirt for your event:

Running shirt material

You need something that is moisture-wicking (draws sweat away from your body) and quick-drying. **Polyester and nylon are in, cotton is out**. Merino wool can be great too for cooler events.

The one drawback with polyester is that it absorbs sweat and is quite stubborn about it, so shirts you use regularly may start to have a little bit of a 'scent' to them.

Sun Protection

I recommend finding a shirt with a UPF rating if you're going running in a warmer country in exposed sunlight. Pick your UPF rating to suit the conditions.

Non-chafing Seams

If you're buying a shirt from a reputable running company, these shouldn't be an issue. **Always do your dress rehearsal** before a big run though, regardless who made your shirt – the last thing you want is uncomfortable rubbing ruining your big day.

Sleeve Length

Long-sleeved shirts can provide extra protection from the sun on warm days, or can keep you warm on colder days, so take this into consideration and gauge the conditions you're likely to experience on your run.

Thickness

In cold weather you may choose to run with two layers, or find a shirt with an inner liner than helps wick away sweat. If running in warm or hot conditions, then go for an ultra-light shirt - any extra thickness is just going to heat you up and add weight.

4-HOUR MARATHON

Compression Shirts

Despite their popularity, most people can't actually quantify exactly what it is that the compression gear does to potentially enhance either performance or recovery.

Some online articles will tell you compression wear has no effect on performance while running – others say that when compression is used correctly, it can improve venous return and help oxygenate working muscles. However, in the case of distance running, this so far seems to have only a very slight increase in performance. So I wouldn't recommend shelling out your cash for compression clothing if you just want to run that little bit faster.

Some people like the feel of compression wear while running – if you're one of these people, then go for it! Minor secondary benefits to running with compression wear is that it can keep you warmer, and reduce chafing (but hopefully you've already eliminated the possibility of chafing using other methods).

Colour

Lighter colours absorb less heat from the sun, so white is never a bad idea. Lighter colours are also *more visible in darkness*, which may be worth bearing in mind if you're training in the early morning or late evening. Same goes for shirts with reflective strips.

Accessory pockets

There are a few shirts on the market with pockets built in at various places, usually around the lower back, for stashing your gels / salts / keys in. These can be useful in runs where you're lacking storage space and don't want to take a big pack. As always, train with the shirt beforehand and make sure the pocket load doesn't bounce around, chafe, or rub.

Running Shorts

Here's what to consider when selecting running shorts:

Material

You need something that is moisture-wicking (draws sweat away from your body) and quick-drying. Like shirts, polyester and nylon are good options.

Pockets

If you can get a pair of shorts with a small zip-pocket (preferably right at the back), then go for it. The additional weight and cost of getting the pocket is worth it for being able to easily store and access a couple of gels, salts, iPods, etc. on runs when you don't take a pack.

Compression Shorts

As mentioned in our shirts section, the effectiveness of compression gear seems to depend on who is wearing it. Many people enjoy the 'lightly massaging' feeling of wearing compression shorts, and feel it aides with muscle recovery.

Minor secondary benefits to running with compression wear are that it can keep you warmer, and reduce chafing (but hopefully you've already eliminated the possibility of chafing using other methods).

Liner and Seams

Liners and seams exist so you don't have to wear underwear, thus preventing chafing. However, when running long distances it's still a good idea to apply a lubricant, like Bodyglide, down there. If you're buying shorts from a reputable running company, chafing seams shouldn't be an issue. Always do your dress rehearsal before a big run though, regardless who made your shorts.

Length

I'd never suggest you commit sins against decency while running a race, but shorter shorts can make a difference – especially in heat. The longer the shorts, the more heat and moisture will hang around your nether regions, which can lead to discomfort, chafing and rashes.

Running Pack

Many marathon runners, myself included, choose to run with a pack. When you consider the items you might want to carry with you – gels, iPhone, keys, drinks bottle – it makes a lot of sense to take something to carry all these in.

I opt for a 'vest' style pack – it is practically a waistcoat covered in handy pockets. It means that anything you carry is held close to your body and doesn't bounce around.

Some runners opt for a waist-pack, but over long distances I find these bounce on the hips a bit too much, and affect my running gait.

Choosing to run with a running pack is very much personal preference, depending on how many things you are carrying with you, and how comfortable you are with one. My personal recommendation is to get a lightweight one with lots of pockets – no need for a hydration pack in the back, these are just cumbersome and not easy to refill on the course.

Hats

Running with a hat can be a preference, but most runners will throw one on to keep the sun off their face and out of their eyes, and their hair in one place.

If the sun is going to be out, take a hat. If you're out for a few hours, that's a lot of sun exposure. Covering your head and face can keep you shaded and psychologically keep that *"I'm getting baked here"* feeling away.

A soft, wide-brimmed hat with a neck-string works very well – and can even be filled with water and dunked over your head at aid stations.

Hats can help absorb some sweat, but I recommend taking a buff to efficiently wipe away your sweat from your head.

Sunglasses

Running-specific sunglasses can cost over $200, if you are taking things seriously. I'm here to tell you shouldn't have to spend as much as $50 on a new pair – in fact, you've probably got a pair floating around the house that are sufficient. It's nice to have a pair of 'sports' sunglasses, but your old Aviators or Oakleys may well do the trick if you're cash-strapped.

Things to look for:

4-HOUR MARATHON

UV protection

UVA and UVB protection should be the baseline requirement when shopping for new shades.

Comfortable when running

Can you wear them during a long run without them bouncing around or causing discomfort?

Weight

There is a near-negligible difference between a pair of ultra-light sports shades and your buddy's new Ray-ban Wayfarers, so don't let this play a factor when the salesperson is giving his sales pitch.

Getting Technical

Other things that you might look for on a pair of sports sunglasses, but are 'nice to haves' – shatter-resistant material, interchangeable lenses, anti-fog lenses, vented sides, polarised lenses . . . but don't get too hung up on them.

4-HOUR MARATHON

Chapter 5: Nutrition and

Hydration

Nutrition and Fuelling

The reason you eat while you run is to convert food into energy to fuel your exercise – therefore, you want to select foods that:

i) Can quickly and easily be digested and turned into energy,

ii) Have a high calorie content – calorific value is a direct measurement of energy in food,

iii) Assuming you are carrying this food, you want it to be lightweight, or have the highest calorie to weight ratio possible,

iv) Be edible in the conditions you are running in – if you're going for a race in a hot climate, you want something you can still stomach after 4 hrs in 30°C heat!

Fuelling Strategy

Developing a good fuelling strategy – or planning what to eat, and how often – is key to your performance in a distance running event.

The first thing to note is that everyone is different – people have different tastes, digestive abilities and preferences. Some runners will fuel a run with a high-sugar gel every 40 minutes without missing a beat, others will go all day on the banana they chomped down at the start line. Experimenting during training and finding out what suits you is essential.

Eating when running is hard.
Especially when you've been running long distances, and when it's hot outside. Suddenly, that Clif bar is like a leaden block in your hand, and no amount of chewing is going to make it go down.

I generally recommend having some type of fuel every hour – be it a gel or a handful of nuts.

Experienced runners survive on one gel every 30-40 minutes for the duration of a marathon, while many other distance runners will only eat very 3-4 hours on the trail, or when they feel hungry.

Having a strategy and sticking to it is important – this way you will be constantly fuelling your body at the rate you are comfortable with. Going off-script halfway through a race is never a good idea!

Gels

These syrupy sweet wonderpacks are specifically designed for athletic performance, delivering instant energy to your body. They typically are a mix of maltodexterin and fructose (plus added flavours) which both can be processed quickly into fuel.

Most gel users take them for any event of two hours or more. They typically give you a 100 calorie, +-40 minute energy boost, so most manufacturers recommend taking one every 40 minutes – that is, if you can stomach the sticky sweetness of them!

That's one of the main drawbacks of gels – they taste like a synthetically sweetened honey. If you can get past that, they can be an ideal fuel form. Some people need a drink with them to wash down the gels.

Some gels have added caffeine – this can be your friend in long runs, but trial them before using them on a race.

And gels come in different consistencies – some are more watery than others (high5 for example), which help you swallow them.

Few of us can handle 7+ gels in a row, so it's important to mix up your race snacking.

Other Snacks - Trail Mix, Peanuts, Potato Chips / Crisps, Pretzels

Maybe you can't stomach gels, or prefer something a little more natural. Whatever the case, when you're choosing snacks for running fuel **you want to focus on the calories per gram**. Trail mix, natural energy bars, peanuts and so on have about the highest calorie per gram ratio of anything out there – and they tend to be exactly what your body craves a few hours into a run! Crushing up pretzels and chips are a great way to make them fit into a smaller space, and easier to eat while running too.

Hydration

Keeping yourself hydrated is important during your marathon, but that doesn't mean you should just drink as much water as you can. Drinking too much can lead to stomach slosh, or – much worse – hyponatremia, if you mess up your salt balance.

Likewise, dehydration during a run can lead to medical issues, cramp, and certainly doesn't do your kidneys any good.

The medical advice on hydration in marathons and endurance events continues to evolve. It's been quoted recently that more people have died of over-hydration than dehydration during athletic events.

With this in mind, the current medical advice for performing activities where you sweat a lot is to drink enough to quench your thirst – i.e. just enough to avoid getting thirsty[2].

Your GI tract can only process 700-750ml / hr, so bear in mind that drinking anything more than this will lead to the excess fluid sloshing around in your stomach.

As with every aspect of distance running, the trick with keeping your hydration balanced is in the training – experiment with different quantities when you go for a run, and find out what suits you.

---

[2] https://www.medicalnewstoday.com/articles/313389.php

4-HOUR MARATHON

Water should be consumed gradually and continuously over a run, in small sips rather than large volumes.

Using a hat to keep the sun off you can aid with sun exposure and preventing dehydration.

4-HOUR MARATHON

Chapter 6: Before the Marathon

Preparation is everything, and whatever your training schedule looks like, there are a few things you want to prepare for at various milestones before the marathon.

In this section, I cover everything you should be concerned about in the final four weeks before your big day.

Four weeks out is roughly the stage where you want to start tapering, and although your training commitments will be winding down, there's still a lot to think about and prepare for your marathon.

The trick is to get to the start line in the most prepared and more physically ready state possible – to give yourself the best chance possible of getting around those 26.2 miles comfortably. This means everything from travel plans, to what you should eat, to how you pin your bib onto your t-shirt . . . you don't want to be leaving any of these factors to last-minute chance.

You want to wake up on the day of your marathon feeling well-rested, prepared and knowing exactly what you are going to be doing at every step of the way before the race starts. This is where all your planning and training pays off – running a marathon is really the celebration of all the training you've put in – it's the 'victory lap' of all the hard hours you've put in over the past few months.

So, in this section, we'll go through certain things you want to consider at four weeks before the race, one week before the race, the night before the race and the morning of the race.

If you follow the steps included here you should reach the start line calm, rested, and ready to take on those 26.2 miles to the absolute best of your ability.

Four Weeks Before the Marathon

It's four weeks before your marathon and your training at its peak – at some point this week you should be starting to taper, if you haven't already. It's around this point you will do your longest run – the longest distance you'll cover by foot prior to the marathon.

Besides your long runs and tapering, it's time to consider some other aspects of your preparation. Here's what you want to cover, about a month before the marathon:

Dress Rehearsals

At least once before your race, you've got to go out and do a long run in all the gear you intend to wear during the actual event. You should schedule this for at least a month before your race to allow time for changing anything. This 'dry run' will identify any kinks in your approach before the big race.

Wear every piece of gear you plan to run with. This means hat, sunglasses, shirt, hydration system. The idea is to mimic the conditions of your actual race as best you can.

If you are planning to tape or lubricate your feet before the race, do the same on your Dress Rehearsal.

4-HOUR MARATHON

If you are wearing a pack or a waist-belt, you can learn a lot about how best to pack your backpack so there's nothing too sharp or uncomfortable rubbing against your back. Sometimes these little things only manifest themselves after 2-3hrs of continuous running.

Food, hydration and salts - whatever your hydration/salt/gel/snack programme is, now is the time to trial it. Get used to using your watch to fuel and hydrate on a regular basis. By now you should also have a hydration / fuelling schedule in mind – now is the time to trial it for any hiccups.

Do you have the space required to carry everything you want to – be it pockets, a waist belt, a vest? Decide now what you will keep in each one – things like snacks, gels, salts, money, hand sanitizer, etc. and test out the system.

Prepare by thinking of all the eventualities that could happen out on the marathon:

- What if I have a bad stomach and need to use a bathroom?

- What if I get injured and need to get a taxi or ride back to the finish?

- What if that nagging knee injury comes back – can I tape it up mid-race? Should I bring tape?

4-HOUR MARATHON

Study the Route

If you haven't already, now is the time to seriously start studying the marathon route. You should already have figured out what the terrain and gradients are going to be like, but now it's time to get familiar with the actual route. You want to look at things like:

- Where is the start and finish lines? And how do you get there / leave? Are they closing access roads for the race (in which case transport might be a bit more complex)? Are the start line and finish line in different locations?

- Can you have a drop bag? (A bag of personal belongings which you hand in at the start of the race and collect at the end). What are the arrangements?

- The frequency and location of any inclines. Hopefully you're already aware of any hills on the route, but now is the time to look at where they actually occur – if the one big hill on the course is at 37km, you want to keep something in the tank for that one. An even pace is recommended throughout, but it there are significant hills along the way then it often pays to be tactical and slow down (or even walk – with big strides) up the hill.

- Frequency and stock of any aid stations. Some races have aid stations every kilometre, some races every 10km. As a minimum the aid station will supply water, but if you're lucky and running a well-supported race you might find snacks, isotonic drinks and chocolates. Now is the time to familiarise yourself with the aid stations – where you'll find them and what they will supply, so you can plan accordingly.

- Medical support. We all hope we'll never need it, but you should check out what kind of medical support is available – and where you'll find it. There will almost certainly be some form of medical tent at the end of the race, but it's worth finding out what is available along the way – will there be a medic at each aid station? Every 10km? Best have an idea before you start, just in case something goes wrong.

Race Registration

Check out the marathon's website, and familiarise yourself with the race registration process. This is not 'signing up' for the race – that took place a few months ago – this is the part where you go and pick up your race bib, often with an ID check to confirm it's really you. Some races simply mail you out the bib, and others hand you your bib on the day of the race.

These vary depending on the size of the event, but often take place the weekend before the marathon, and sometimes the day before. Often bigger 'city marathons' will have a big race expo with stands and promotions, where they also distribute the bibs.

Travel Plans

One month out is when you want to have your travel plans fully firmed up. This obviously varies a lot depending on the race location and size of the event, but it's always good to have your travel and accommodation plans mapped out well in advance. Usually the organiser's website can help you with travel tips and hotel recommendations.

Some tips:

- Hotels. Running a big city marathon? Try and book that hotel as far in advance as possible. Hotels within limping distance of the finishing line will be flooded with requests for the marathon weekend, and may well raise their prices. Check them out as soon as you can. Another tip: swimming, and floundering around in a pool, is a great way to relax and soothe your legs after a marathon. If it's an option, find a hotel with a pool.

- Travel. Again, generally the earlier you can make your travel plans the better.   This is especially true if you're running a marathon in some exotic location which is only served by one plane / train per day – assume that all the runners will be using the same mode of transport as you, and book early.

Fuelling and Nutrition Strategy

I've already covered marathon fuelling earlier, but needless to say you should have trialled everything you plan to eat several times before the marathon.

Now, four weeks out, you should have a good idea of your fuelling strategy – whether it's to eat a gel every hour, or simply to have a banana at the start line – now is the time to get that strategy pegged down.

4-HOUR MARATHON

Don't Do Anything New

Your body is at its peak right now, and the next four weeks is simply about preserving it and resting it.

For that reason, now is not the time to take up Muay Thai boxing, or to decide you want to start a trendy new diet. If you can, don't plan any serious travel for the month before the marathon.

Stick to what has been working, keep your head down and follow the tapering laid out in your training plan. The last thing you want at this point is to get injured or ill. Look after yourself; you're getting close to the start line!

One Week Before the Marathon

Alright, now the marathon is practically in your sights. You've spent the previous few weeks tapering, and by now you should be feeling rested and prepared. This week is all about looking after yourself, and getting to the start line in optimal condition.

Keep Looking After Yourself

Now you're in the final countdown, it's critical to look after yourself this week.

Getting ill this week can completely kill your marathon plans – even if you recover enough to attempt the marathon, you are still sacrificing all your training.

If that colleague you sit next to starts coughing, move away from them. Take extra care with personal hygiene, and only eat quality foods from places you really trust. If in doubt, cook yourself.

Plan Out The 48hrs Before the Race

One week before the marathon, sit down and run through the 48hrs before the race. Where are you going to stay, how are you going to get to the start line, which clothes are you going to take with you, and so on. Clearly picture in your head every part of the build-up to the race, then the race itself and the period after the race.

Run (a Little)

As per your training plan, you want to run a little. You should do an abridged "long run" one week before the marathon, then short training runs that are just there to keep your legs limber and loose, so they're ready come race day.

Stretch (But Don't Do Anything New)

It's likely that you've incorporated some cross-training into your tapering period, and that's great. It fills in the gaps in your training schedule as you wind down your running training, and keeps your body active.

If your cross-training includes pilates, yoga or gym work, that's great – just make sure you aren't incorporating anything new into your training at this point.

If the instructor decides to take you through a complex leg stretch, or asks you to push a bit harder when working on the hamstrings, just politely explain you've got a big race coming up so are being delicate with your legs.

Rest and Eat

This week, you're allowed to relax a bit more. 'Carb loading' is a favourite of all marathoners – eating carb-rich foods this week will give your body more fuel to burn through on race day.

Note that fuelling strategies differ, and especially these days not every runner conforms with the 'carb-loading' programmes that used to be standard. If you're a beginner, it won't hurt to stick to hearty evening meals with some pasta.

Doctors say that it's **most important to get a good sleep two nights before the race**, so if your marathon is on a Sunday, make sure you give yourself the best possible rest on Friday night.

The Day Before

By now you should have completed race registration, have all your equipment, clothing and bags looked out, know exactly what your travel arrangements before and after the race are going to look like . . . you should be ready to eat those 26.2 miles.

What to Eat

Avoid caffeine if you can. The night before a race, you're likely to be nervous enough as it is – adding any stimulants to your body won't help. Avoid alcohol too – there'll be plenty of time for that on the other side of the 26.2 miles.

Unless you're following a set dietary plan, I advise you eat heartily – without over-eating. Stick to carb-rich foods to give your body fuel. Don't eat a huge plate of meat just before going to bed – in fact, try to eat at least 3-4 hours before bed.

Prepare Everything

Alright, here are the final steps. You're getting your gear together for the final time before you put it on tomorrow morning. The trick is to do everything that you can possibly do the day before the race, to minimise your workload - and panic - on the morning of the race.

Here's exactly what you want to do:

- Set two alarms. You're getting up early, but you still want some good sleep. If nothing else, setting two alarms gives you a lot of reassurance that you're not going to sleep in.

- Set out everything you need. This means running shoes, socks, shorts, shirt, hat, GPS watch, food, salts, money, iPod – have it all neatly laid out, so when you get up in the morning you simply have to put it all on.

- Ensure your phone and GPS watch are plugged in and charging.

- Plan what to eat pre-race. This is cover in the next few pages, but you should have it prepared the night before.

- Pin your bib to your race shirt. You don't want to be nervously pinning the bib on in the morning before the race, so do it the night before. Tip: it's easiest to pin these in place while wearing the shirt.

Revise the Race Information

It's good to check over all the tiny details again, one more time. Check what time you're meant to arrive at the start line, remind yourself where the aid stations are, what is available at the finish line, and so on.

The Morning of the Race

Here it is, the big day!

You should have everything laid out and ready to go, so you simply wake up, wash and go.

Race Day Checklist

Here's a checklist of the essentials – and some optional items – to check for race day:

- Running shoes
- Shorts
- Shirt
- Socks
- Hat
- Sunglasses
- Gloves, if cold
- Extra clothing layer, if cold
- Running vest / pack, if required
- Suncream, especially on your face and back of your neck
- Lubricant / anti-chafe cream on your feet, thighs and nipples (band-aids also work on nipples)
- Race bib
- Safety pins
- Gels, drinks, snacks
- Medication, if required.

4-HOUR MARATHON

What to Eat

Your goals for eating before a running event should be:

i)   eat something that will fuel your event
ii)   don't try anything new or exotic
iii)   don't eat anything that might unsettle your stomach.

Typically, in the hours before the race starts people will eat light. Before your event you should have prepared sufficiently that you know what your body can accept and process before a long run.

Examples are porridge / oatmeal, bananas, or smoothies. Smoothies are a great way to throw several fuel sources together – bananas, nuts, seeds, peanut butter – and turn them into an easy-to-digest drink!

As long as your stomach allows it, you should each something solid at least two hours before the race starts – as marathons usually start early in the morning, you may wish to eat as soon as you wake up.

Warming Up

Most races start early in the morning, so you're likely to have just gotten out of bed and made your way to the start line. For this reason, it's a good idea to do something to let your legs warm up a little before you start.

This means power-walking to the marathon, and doing some light jogging repeats in the 30 minutes before the race starts, to get your legs ready.

Go to the Toilet

Even if you went to the toilet 30 minutes earlier, there's a good chance you'll unexpectedly realise you need to go just before the start line. Pre-race jitters gets to everybody, and there are often lines at the facilities in the 20 minutes before the race kicks off – a lot of nervous stomachs! Factor in a trip to the bathroom, and if in doubt perhaps bring along some wet wipes too, just in case.

Last minute fuelling

The 30 minutes before the race starts is quite a good time to have any last-minute snacks – be it sweets, crisps or a gel. Food takes an absolute minimum of 15 minutes to be converted into fuel by your body, so plan accordingly.

Chapter 7: During the

Marathon

Finally, the main event is here!

The months of training are about to pay off – you should look at the actual marathon as a celebration of your months of hard work – it's finally here, and you're ready to kill it!

If you've followed this guide so far, then your marathon will be a smooth and enjoyable experience – a culmination of the hours of running you've put in, and the preparation you've invested in.

Therefore, this section covers things that you might experience during your marathon, and how you'd deal with them. They're written from experience and hopefully give you an insight into what to expect.

The Start Line

Start lines can be busy, crowded places. In big races, runners are divided into groups based on their projected finish times. My tip is to try and get close to the start of your group 'area', to minimise getting caught up in the herd. In the huge city marathons such as London and New York, it's typical that your first 20-30 minutes are simply done at a walking pace due to the density of the runners around you. So ideally you want to find some space, and the best place to do that is usually right at the front of your group.

Don't worry if you feel you're lining up with faster runners – don't be intimidated, they'll take off right at the start and leave you to run your own race. Just do your best not to get swamped by a mass of runners.

Gun Time vs. Chip Time

Most races these days record your time via 'chip time' – this is done by a little microchip that they put either in your bib or attach to your shoe, and it accurately records exactly when you cross the start and finish lines. This way, if you're in a huge crowd when the race starts and it takes you five minutes to even cross the start line, then this time is not counted.

'Gun Time' is your time from the official start of the race, i.e. when the flag is dropped or the gun is fired. Although your gun time may be recorded, your chip time is much more accurate and is the one that you and the race organisers will quote at the end of the race as your 'official time.'

Don't Forget Your GPS

So many runners simply forget to start their GPS watches at the start line of a race. They get swept up in the atmosphere, then look at their wrist after a couple of miles and curse that they forgot to turn it on.

Don't let this be you. Remember to switch on your GPS watch in good time before the start in order to find a GPS signal, and remember to 'start' to record your run when your race starts – usually this will be when you cross the start line and go over the timing mat (i.e. recording your chip time, as opposed to your gun time). Tip: when your lining up at the start line, keep your thumb over the 'START" button of your GPS watch to ensure you don't forget to push it.

Pace (A Reminder)

Why am I bringing up pace again?

Because no matter how well trained you are, at the start line is it very easy to be overcome by adrenaline and confidence and ditch your strategy altogether. It happens all the time, and usually to ill-effect.

Take a second to remind yourself of your goal – to comfortably complete a marathon in under four hours – and stick to the plan. Use the 4-hr marathon pace and you'll kill it. If you're feeling the urge to speed up, keep it in the back pocket for the last five miles.

Getting Swept Along

Alright, one more point on pacing that I want to flag up.

In a big marathon event it's likely that you'll experience the sensation of being 'swept along' during the first few miles.

This is when the atmosphere and adrenaline take over, and you feel yourself gliding down the road alongside the other runners, with no regard for pace – it just *feels* easy, it feels great!

This can be a great experience – at least for a short while – but remember to check in with your GPS. It's not uncommon to be getting swept along and end up running a full minute/mile faster than you think you are – when everything feels so light and breezy, you just feel like you can keep going forever.

Remember you are running a consistent pace – check your GPS, remind yourself that you've still got a long way ahead of you, and try to stick to your target pace – it might feel a little like you're throwing the brakes on, but your body will thank you in the latter stages of the marathon.

Crowds, Support and Music

In a similar vein to being 'swept along', crowds of supporters and family / friends can have a surprising effect on your performance. Hearing people shout your name, or seeing them clap and cheer you on can really give you a boost, in a similar way to listening to your favourite upbeat songs can.

On that note, if you feel like listening to music during your marathon, that's great – there are studies that prove it can help with cardiovascular performance. Just remember that in certain situations they can be a personal risk if you can't hear other people, or vehicles around you. At the end of the day, part of the experience of a marathon can be soaking in the atmosphere, and listening to music may remove you slightly from the present. Personally, when I take my music player to a race I save it for the last 10km, where I know I'm going to have to dig deep.

Eating

Remember your fuelling strategy on the day.

4-HOUR MARATHON

It's likely you'll be offered food along the way – this could be sweets, fruit, isotonic drinks, or just about anything else. If you feel like eating it, then go for it – but bear in mind not to deviate too far from your own fuelling strategy.

For example, eating a banana during a marathon can be a huge mistake if you haven't done this during training – they can lead to stomach cramps. Same goes for energy gels – if you haven't trained with them, it's unwise to wait until marathon day to experiment with them. They give many experienced athletes upset stomachs, so learn what works for your body well in advance of the marathon.

The other thing to bear in mind is to match your fuelling strategy to the marathon course – if the course is flat and dull, then you can space out your fuelling evenly. If there's a big hill at the 23-mile mark however, you want to plan to fuel up in preparation for that obstacle.

Aid Stations

Aid stations are a welcome method of support, providing water and often snacks and medical help. Make sure you've researched exactly what is being provided at the aid stations before you set off.

Some bigger marathons have aid stations that provide muscle-relaxing sprays, cold wet sponges, etc. Check these out beforehand and assess whether they're a good idea – don't just stop and get the muscle spray if you don't feel you need it.

The number one rule for aid stations should be – **don't stop**. If you stop and stand still, or worse, sit down, then starting moving again is exponentially harder. When you reach an aid station, keep running, or walking if you have to, and grab the snacks and water as you move.

Toilets

Try and get an idea where there are going to be toilets on the route before you start your race. It's common to get a nervous stomach during your marathon, and even if your tummy has handled gels and sports nutrition well during training, things can change on the day itself. Having an idea where the toilets are gives you plenty of time to plan ahead.

Hitting The Wall

Hitting the wall is a common occurrence in first marathons, especially if you're underprepared.

Hitting the wall means reaching physical exhaustion – it's when your body stops co-operating and starts telling you to stop. Your muscles' glycogen levels are bottoming out. It makes every single step five times harder – rather than gliding forward, now every single pace requires some exertion of will power, to overcome your body's desires to stop.

Proper pacing and fuelling with sports drinks and gels can prevent your glycogen levels from vanishing to zero.

Usually, it hits you in the final 5-7 miles of the marathon, and doesn't go away. Your upper legs will typically become heavy and be very reluctant to move. You'll find it very hard to muster energy to do anything other than walk at an average pace, and mentally you'll be feeling rather low.

4-HOUR MARATHON

The bad news is that pushing through 'the wall' will make your body sore the next day – it's telling you it's time to stop, and you're telling it that it has to keep going.

It can be easy to reach this stage and feel like you should stop – you've given it your best shot, but your body has said no, and you feel terrible – everything would be so much easier if you just stopped now.

The trick to overcoming the wall is to remind yourself exactly how far you've got left – probably only a handful of miles at best, and that you've covered this distance dozens of times during training. Remind yourself that no matter what happens, you can still walk to the finish line – and if that's all you're capable of, that's what you'll do. You might lose a little bit of your ego along the way, but what's important is finishing, not getting across the line under a specific time.

Hitting the wall is horrible, and runners who experience this have a much tougher day than those who glide to the finish line. But at the same time, the reasons you've hit the wall are rarely severe enough to justify stopping – it becomes a mental game, so get your game face on and plough through.

Hot Spots

Hot spots are any kind of ache of pain in your feet experienced while running. Often, they're an early indicator of the onset of blisters, so it's important to be aware of them.

Assuming you've prepared sufficiently and trained in the same socks and shoes that you are doing the marathon in, it's unlikely you'll experience any serious hot spot issues. You may develop some pain towards the end of the marathon, once you're into 'virgin mileage' – but by that point, you can push through it.

If you do experience hot spots, then you should at least consider what could be causing them. It's totally dependent on the scenario – how much pain you have, how quickly it has developed, and how far into your marathon you are.

Does it feel like it could just be some bunched-up socks rubbing against your sole? If it comes on quickly, then that's probably what it is. In this case, it's usually worth stopping for a second and trying to un-bunch your sock – you might even be able to do this without taking your shoes off.

If it seems to be something more severe, then it's up to you whether to stop and address it, or continue onwards. If it feels like something is in your shoe / sock – like a stone or piece of grit, then it's worth checking this out and seeing if you can clear it.

If it just seems like the onset of a blister caused by regular running, then there's little you can do during the marathon. Even if you wanted to drain the blister, it's unlikely you'd be able to do it in a hygienic manner (let alone have something to pop it). In tough circumstances, people have used the pins on their bibs to pop blisters - but this runs the risk of infecting the blister.

With any hot spots during a marathon, bear in mind that if you can get to the finish line, you can address them later – no matter how hideous they are. It might not be pretty, but sometimes persevering with blisters is the best option available.

4-HOUR MARATHON

Sore Shoulders

This is a common complaint during marathons. The act of running actually uses a little bit of your upper body, and your shoulders can start to get tired. Bear in mind that this is fairly common towards the end of a marathon, and don't let it trouble you too much.

Painkillers in Marathons

It's fairly common to take painkillers during marathons – they help dull the pain caused by fatigue in your legs.

If you're considering taking painkillers as a preventative measure, I'd recommend taking a maximum of two – one at the start, and one in the latter stages. If you're not sure if you need them, don't take them – simple. You may want to keep one in a pocket for the latter stages, but plan not to take it.

An important note is the type of painkillers you should take during a marathon – stick to Paracetamol (other brand names: Tylenol, Panadol, Anacin, etc). You should avoid any kind of anti-inflammatory medication during a marathon (Ibuprofen, Aspirin, Advil, Nurofin, etc.). This type of painkiller really taxes your kidneys, and during an endurance event where you're already sweating a lot, possibly de-hydrated and working your kidneys, the last thing you want is to stress them more.

As an aside, once you've finished the marathon, had some water and relaxed, then it is safe to take anti-inflammatories. But while running – stick to a paracetamol.

(Note: bear in mind the medical note at the start of this book. Don't take anything without running it by a doctor first).

When Injuries Occur

No matter how much you train and prepare, there's always the chance of an injury occurring during your marathon.

What to do?

If it's a sudden pain, for example a sharp pain in the leg, then you should stop running – walk for a while and see what happens. If there is medical help at the next aid station, then seek advice.

If you're experiencing a dull ache or growing pain, then only run when you feel you can – otherwise see if walking can help.

Dealing with injuries during a marathon is not easy, and the circumstances change based on the nature of the injury and how far into the marathon you are.

I'd suggest that if you're injured and you think that continuing to run could cause lasting damage to your body, stop running – at least walk. See if any medical support is available, and weigh up what your likelihood of finishing is against the potential damage you could cause to your body.

4-HOUR MARATHON

The Art of the DNF

DNF = "Did Not Finish".

This is what the race organiser will put against your 'race time' field in the event that you drop out.

It's a horrible thought to consider that after all your training, you'll drop out for some reason, but consider this – **almost every serious distance runner has had at least one DNF in their running career**.

Maybe their stomach gave out during the race. Maybe that old nagging knee injury re-appeared at the half-way point, and put their PB attempt to bed. Maybe they'd been fighting off a flu the week leading up to the race. Maybe they weren't as prepared as they assumed they were.

Whatever the reason behind it, the point is that DNF's can happen to anybody. The trick is to use a DNF as motivation to get back up and re-attempt next time. Did your legs give out on mile 21 this year?

Then good news - you've got a full 12 months to prepare and get ready to kill the same race next year.

4-HOUR MARATHON

Chapter 8: After the Marathon

You've made it!

You've managed to get yourself across the finish line, hopefully smiling and giving the camera a thumbs up.

Most of what I'm going to tell you in this section is general advice to help you recover faster – but the main thing you care about is that you've just finished your first marathon!

I realise your priorities are likely to be beer and burgers . . .

Anyway, here are some things to bear in mind:

Keep Moving

If you managed to run all the way to the finish line, that's fantastic. But beware, that lactic acid is waiting in the wings to jump in and stiffen up your legs as soon as you stop moving. So - walk around for a good 15 minutes or so once you cross the finish line – don't sit down and let those legs go stiff.

Walk over to collect your medal, walk to the burger stall, whatever – just don't be too quick to flake out, or you will find it much harder to get up again.

Drink and Eat

Continue to drink water when you finish – your legs may have stopped racing, but your internal organs haven't.

And eat – preferably something as substantial and hearty as you can stomach. It helps kick-start your body's recover process. Something with high protein content is advised.

Elevate Your Legs and Stretch

Once you've walked off the stiffness, grab a seat on the floor and raise your legs up on a chair or wall – this helps drain the excess fluid from them, preventing them from becoming too stiff or swollen. If you can, remain here for twenty minutes of so, and do some gentle stretching – you'll be grateful for it in the coming days, trust me!

Physio and Massage

Better than stretching yourself is getting someone else to do it for you. Likewise, getting a leg massage can really help relieve your tired leg muscles. Some of the bigger marathons organise post-race masseuses – if you can get one of these, go for it!

Tend to Blisters

Now is the time to clean up any foot issues you've had. If they're minor, you can usually leave them alone and they'll gradually disappear on their own over a few days. If they're big, or contain blood, you want to drain them hygienically – clean the whole foot first, especially the area around the blister, then pop it with a sterilised needle at three or four points around the perimeter. Let the blister drain, then consider applying some dressing if the skin flap is left loose – your foot won't be ready to lose the old skin yet to keep the area covered and protected.

To the Pool

If you can, get to a swimming pool. They are one of the best ways to recover. Simply walking around the shallow end of a pool can be a great way to treat your legs after a marathon, and doing strokes like the breast stroke can ease your muscles and help with recovery.

Post-Marathon Blues

In the days following your successful marathon, don't be surprised if you feel a little bit melancholic. The reason is that you've just completed a major challenge, a task that took over a large chunk of your life – and now, believe it or not, you miss the sense of achievement and hard work that you got from all the training. Now it's over, and you'll never be able to run another first marathon again.

Bear in mind that you're likely to be physically laid up too – and not just your legs and feet. Running a marathon puts a tremendous stress on the body, and over the next few days your internals will be working overtime to heal your tired muscles and rebuild itself.

This means that your immune system may be depleted, and you may be more susceptible to viruses and bugs.

Use this period to rest up, don't do anything physically demanding and try not to expose yourself unnecessarily to viruses or unsanitary places. Get plenty of sleep, eat some ice cream and congratulate yourself!

The Next Race

Some marathon runners are 'one-and-dones' – they complete their first ever marathon and are satisfied.

Others go home and immediately sign up for the next race. Whichever camp you're in, give yourself a few days to sit back and process the experience. Remember to reflect on the amount of training you've put in, and your new physical powers, and how you'll lose them if you don't keep training regularly.

You've climbed to the top of a mountain and reached its peak, now do you really want to start roll down the other side, or do you want to aim for that next peak – off in the distance – now you're up here, it's suddenly much easier to get there.

Chapter 9: Conclusion

Running a marathon is not for the faint of heart.

It pushes your body to limits otherwise unknown.

It demands a significant block of commitment and eats into your personal life.

Committing to a marathon is committing to prolonged spells of discomfort with no guaranteed reward at the end.

But – if you can put in the hours of discomfort, and avoid the pitfalls of injury or exhaustion – you'll find all the training and pain are redeemed in full on race day.

Some people run a marathon, go straight home and sign up for another one. Other people cross the finish line and go back to their old lives, happy to have completed the challenge but not looking to revisit it any time soon.

Whichever group you fall into, we hope this book has been of some help. I hope you've taken some helpful information from us and, if nothing else, bear in mind two key tenets:

- **Preparation is everything**. Follow the training plan. Plan for every part of the marathon, rehearse running with the same gear and conditions you are going to face in the race, and plan for every contingency.

- **Consistent pace = happy marathon finisher**. The average marathoner goes out too quick and their overall performance and enjoyment suffers because of it. Having the discipline to run at a consistent, achievable pace will pay off in dividends in the later stages of your race

I think you'll find completing a marathon to be a deeply rewarding experience. It is a major achievement that you'll find can positively influence other areas of your life.

If you have any questions, get in touch at hi@marathonhandbook.com and I'll do our best to help you, whether you're looking for shoe advice or a remedy to chafing.

And head over to www.marathonhandbook.com for much more marathon-related articles, race reports and blogs!

And finally, if you've enjoyed this book at all, please don't forget to leave an Amazon review – it really helps!

Thanks and run far,

- Thomas Watson
Marathon Handbook

Appendix – Block Method Sample

As described in the Training chapter, the Block Method is a great way to build up your pace to the '4-hr pace' before you start the actual 20-week plan.

It's important to note that everyone is different with the Block Method, in terms of how long they'll need to stay on each pattern and how quickly they progress through the ranks.

For runners using the Block Method, I recommend a minimum of two runs per week.   Three is optimal.

Once you have completed the Block Method and all your intervals are black, I'd recommend a couple of weeks of 30-minute, 4-hr marathon pace training runs to consolidate your training base before embarking on the 20-week plan.

On the following page, I've given an example Block Method plan.   Remember, it may be too fast or too slow for you. Start at a point that feels comfortable to you, and only progress when you are confident your body is ready for it.

4-HOUR MARATHON

Week 1

Week 2

Week 3

Week 4

Week 5

Week 6

Week 7

Week 8

Week 9

Appendix – Training Plan

Here is a 20-week training plan for a sub 4-hr marathon – in both miles and kilometres.

You can use them as they are, or fine-tune them to your needs based on the earlier chapters of this book.

Download them in fully-customisable Excel-format spreadsheets here:

www.marathonhandbook.com/4hrs

4-hr Marathon Plan – 20 weeks – miles

MARATHON 🏃 HANDBOOK
4-HR MARATHON TRAINING PLAN (miles) // 20 weeks

WEEK	Monday	Tuesday	Wednesday	Thursday	Friday	Saturday	Sunday
1	Rest Day	Training Run 3 miles *8:46 min / mile*	Speed Work 3 x 800m Repeats *7:42 min / mile*	Cross Training 30 - 60 mins	Training Run 3 miles *8:46 min / mile*	Rest Day	Long Run 7 miles *slow pace*
2	Rest Day	Training Run 3 miles *8:46 min / mile*	Speed Work 3 x 800m Repeats *7:42 min / mile*	Cross Training 30 - 60 mins	Training Run 3 miles *8:46 min / mile*	Rest Day	Long Run 8 miles *slow pace*
3	Rest Day	Training Run 3 miles *8:46 min / mile*	Speed Work 4 x 800m Repeats *7:42 min / mile*	Cross Training 30 - 60 mins	Training Run 3 miles *8:46 min / mile*	Rest Day	Long Run 9 miles *slow pace*
4	Rest Day	Training Run 4 miles *8:46 min / mile*	Speed Work 4 x 800m Repeats *7:42 min / mile*	Cross Training 30 - 60 mins	Training Run 4 miles *8:46 min / mile*	Rest Day	Long Run 6 miles *slow pace*
5	Rest Day	Training Run 4 miles *8:46 min / mile*	Speed Work 5 x 800m Repeats *7:42 min / mile*	Cross Training 30 - 60 mins	Training Run 4 miles *8:46 min / mile*	Rest Day	Long Run 11 miles *slow pace*
6	Rest Day	Training Run 4 miles *8:46 min / mile*	Speed Work 5 x 800m Repeats *7:42 min / mile*	Cross Training 30 - 60 mins	Training Run 4 miles *8:46 min / mile*	Rest Day	Long Run 12 miles *slow pace*
7	Rest Day	Training Run 5 miles *8:46 min / mile*	Speed Work 6 x 800m Repeats *7:42 min / mile*	Cross Training 30 - 60 mins	Training Run 5 miles *8:46 min / mile*	Rest Day	Long Run 9 miles *slow pace*
8	Rest Day	Training Run 5 miles *8:46 min / mile*	Speed Work 6 x 800m Repeats *7:42 min / mile*	Cross Training 30 - 60 mins	Training Run 5 miles *8:46 min / mile*	Rest Day	Long Run 15 miles *slow pace*
9	Rest Day	Training Run 5 miles *8:46 min / mile*	Speed Work 7 x 800m Repeats *7:42 min / mile*	Cross Training 30 - 60 mins	Training Run 5 miles *8:46 min / mile*	Rest Day	Long Run 16 miles *slow pace*
10	Rest Day	Training Run 6 miles *8:46 min / mile*	Speed Work 7 x 800m Repeats *7:42 min / mile*	Cross Training 30 - 60 mins	Training Run 6 miles *8:46 min / mile*	Rest Day	Long Run Half Marathon *slow pace*

4-HOUR MARATHON

		Training Run	Speed Work	Cross Training	Training Run		Long Run
11	Rest Day	6 miles	8 x 800m Repeats	30 - 60 mins	6 miles	Rest Day	17 miles
		8:46 min / mile	7:42 min / mile		8:46 min / mile		slow pace
12	Rest Day	Training Run	Speed Work	Cross Training	Training Run	Rest Day	Long Run
		6 miles	8 x 800m Repeats	30 - 60 mins	6 miles		18 miles
		8:46 min / mile	7:42 min / mile		8:46 min / mile		slow pace
13	Rest Day	Training Run	Speed Work	Cross Training	Training Run	Rest Day	Long Run
		6 miles	9 x 800m Repeats	30 - 60 mins	6 miles		14 miles
		8:46 min / mile	7:42 min / mile		8:46 min / mile		slow pace
14	Rest Day	Training Run	Speed Work	Cross Training	Training Run	Rest Day	Long Run
		6 miles	9 x 800m Repeats	30 - 60 mins	6 miles		20 miles
		8:46 min / mile	7:42 min / mile		8:46 min / mile		slow pace
15	Rest Day	Training Run	Speed Work	Cross Training	Training Run	Rest Day	Half Marathon
		7 miles	10 x 800m Repeats	30 - 60 mins	7 miles		sub 2-hr
		8:46 min / mile	7:42 min / mile		8:46 min / mile		8:46 min / mile
16	Rest Day	Training Run	Speed Work	Cross Training	Training Run	Rest Day	Long Run
		7 miles	10 x 800m Repeats	30 - 60 mins	7 miles		21 miles
		8:46 min / mile	7:42 min / mile		8:46 min / mile		slow pace
17	Rest Day	Training Run	Speed Work	Cross Training	Training Run	Rest Day	Long Run
		5 miles	8 x 800m Repeats	30 - 60 mins	5 miles		15 miles
		8:46 min / mile	7:42 min / mile		8:46 min / mile		slow pace
18	Rest Day	Training Run	Speed Work	Cross Training	Training Run	Rest Day	Long Run
		4 miles	4 x 800m Repeats	30 - 60 mins	4 miles		12 miles
		8:46 min / mile	7:42 min / mile		8:46 min / mile		slow pace
19	Rest Day	Training Run	Rest Day	Cross Training	Training Run	Rest Day	Long Run
		3 miles		30 - 60 mins	3 miles		8 miles
		8:46 min / mile			8:46 min / mile		slow pace
20	Rest Day	Training Run	Rest Day	Short Run	Rest Day	Short Run	Marathon
		3 miles		3 miles		2 miles	
		8:46 min / mile		slow pace		slow pace	

4-hr Marathon Plan – 20 weeks – km

MARATHON 🏃 HANDBOOK

4-HR MARATHON TRAINING PLAN (km) // 20 weeks

WEEK	Monday	Tuesday	Wednesday	Thursday	Friday	Saturday	Sunday
1	Rest Day	Training Run 5 km 5:27 min / km	Speed Work 3 x 800m Repeats 4:47 min / km	Cross Training 30 - 60 mins	Training Run 5 km 5:27 min / km	Rest Day	Long Run 11 km slow pace
2	Rest Day	Training Run 5 km 5:27 min / km	Speed Work 3 x 800m Repeats 4:47 min / km	Cross Training 30 - 60 mins	Training Run 5 km 5:27 min / km	Rest Day	Long Run 13 km slow pace
3	Rest Day	Training Run 5 km 5:27 min / km	Speed Work 4 x 800m Repeats 4:47 min / km	Cross Training 30 - 60 mins	Training Run 5 km 5:27 min / km	Rest Day	Long Run 14.5 km slow pace
4	Rest Day	Training Run 6.5 km 5:27 min / km	Speed Work 4 x 800m Repeats 4:47 min / km	Cross Training 30 - 60 mins	Training Run 6.5 km 5:27 min / km	Rest Day	Long Run 9.5 km slow pace
5	Rest Day	Training Run 6.5 km 5:27 min / km	Speed Work 5 x 800m Repeats 4:47 min / km	Cross Training 30 - 60 mins	Training Run 6.5 km 5:27 min / km	Rest Day	Long Run 17.5 km slow pace
6	Rest Day	Training Run 6.5 km 5:27 min / km	Speed Work 5 x 800m Repeats 4:47 min / km	Cross Training 30 - 60 mins	Training Run 6.5 km 5:27 min / km	Rest Day	Long Run 19 km slow pace
7	Rest Day	Training Run 8 km 5:27 min / km	Speed Work 6 x 800m Repeats 4:47 min / km	Cross Training 30 - 60 mins	Training Run 8 km 5:27 min / km	Rest Day	Long Run 14.5 km slow pace
8	Rest Day	Training Run 8 km 5:27 min / km	Speed Work 6 x 800m Repeats 4:47 min / km	Cross Training 30 - 60 mins	Training Run 8 km 5:27 min / km	Rest Day	Long Run 24 km slow pace
9	Rest Day	Training Run 8 km 5:27 min / km	Speed Work 7 x 800m Repeats 4:47 min / km	Cross Training 30 - 60 mins	Training Run 8 km 5:27 min / km	Rest Day	Long Run 26 km slow pace
10	Rest Day	Training Run 9.5 km 5:27 min / km	Speed Work 7 x 800m Repeats 4:47 min / km	Cross Training 30 - 60 mins	Training Run 9.5 km 5:27 min / km	Rest Day	Long Run Half Marathon slow pace

4-HOUR MARATHON

		Training Run	Speed Work	Cross Training	Training Run		Long Run
11	Rest Day	9.5 km	8 x 800m Repeats	30 - 60 mins	9.5 km	Rest Day	27 km
		5:27 min / km	4:47 min / km		5:27 min / km		slow pace
12	Rest Day	Training Run	Speed Work	Cross Training	Training Run	Rest Day	Long Run
		9.5 km	8 x 800m Repeats	30 - 60 mins	9.5 km		29 km
		5:27 min / km	4:47 min / km		5:27 min / km		slow pace
13	Rest Day	Training Run	Speed Work	Cross Training	Training Run	Rest Day	Long Run
		9.5 km	9 x 800m Repeats	30 - 60 mins	9.5 km		22.5 km
		5:27 min / km	4:47 min / km		5:27 min / km		slow pace
14	Rest Day	Training Run	Speed Work	Cross Training	Training Run	Rest Day	Long Run
		9.5 km	9 x 800m Repeats	30 - 60 mins	9.5 km		32 km
		5:27 min / km	4:47 min / km		5:27 min / km		slow pace
15	Rest Day	Training Run	Speed Work	Cross Training	Training Run	Rest Day	Half Marathon
		11 km	10 x 800m Repeats	30 - 60 mins	11 km		sub 2-hr
		5:27 min / km	4:47 min / km		5:27 min / km		5:27 min / km
16	Rest Day	Training Run	Speed Work	Cross Training	Training Run	Rest Day	Long Run
		11 km	10 x 800m Repeats	30 - 60 mins	11 km		34 km
		5:27 min / km	4:47 min / km		5:27 min / km		slow pace
17	Rest Day	Training Run	Speed Work	Cross Training	Training Run	Rest Day	Long Run
		8 km	8 x 800m Repeats	30 - 60 mins	8 km		24 km
		5:27 min / km	4:47 min / km		5:27 min / km		slow pace
18	Rest Day	Training Run	Speed Work	Cross Training	Training Run	Rest Day	Long Run
		6.5 km	4 x 800m Repeats	30 - 60 mins	6.5 km		19 km
		5:27 min / km	4:47 min / km		5:27 min / km		slow pace
19	Rest Day	Training Run	Rest Day	Cross Training	Training Run	Rest Day	Long Run
		5 km		30 - 60 mins	5 km		13 km
		5:27 min / km			5:27 min / km		slow pace
20	Rest Day	Training Run	Rest Day	Short Run	Rest Day	Short Run	Marathon
		5 km		5 km		3 km	
		5:27 min / km		slow pace		slow pace	

Made in the USA
Las Vegas, NV
03 May 2022

48364464R00080